DISCRIMINATION
and
DISPARITIES

DISCRIMINATION
and
DISPARITIES

THOMAS SOWELL

BASIC BOOKS

New York

Basic Books
Hachette Book Group
1290 Avenue of the Americas, New York, NY 10104
www.basicbooks.com

Printed in the United States of America
First Edition: March 2018
Published by Basic Books, an imprint of Perseus Books, LLC, a subsidiary of Hachette Book Group, Inc. The Basic Books name and logo is a trademark of the Hachette Book Group.

The publisher is not responsible for websites (or their content) that are not owned by the publisher.

Library of Congress Control Number: 2018931583

ISBNs: 978-1-5416-4560-8 (hardcover), 978-1-5416-4562-2 (ebook)

LSC-C

10 9 8 7 6 5 4 3 2 1

To Professor Walter E. Williams,

who has labored in the same vineyard.

C O N T E N T S

Chapter 1

DISPARITIES and

PREREQUISITES

The fact that economic and other outcomes often differ greatly among individuals, groups, institutions and nations poses questions to which many people give very different answers. At one end of a spectrum of explanations offered is the belief that those who have been less fortunate in their outcomes are genetically less capable. At the other end of the spectrum is the belief that those less fortunate are victims of other people who are more fortunate. In between, there are many other explanations offered. But, whatever the particular explanation offered, there seems to be general agreement that the disparities found in the real world differ greatly from what might be expected by random chance.

Yet the great disparities in outcomes found in economic and other endeavors need not be due to either comparable disparities in innate capabilities or comparable disparities in the way people are treated by other people. The disparities can also reflect the plain fact that success in many kinds of endeavors depends on prerequisites peculiar to each endeavor— and a relatively small difference in meeting those prerequisites can mean a very large difference in outcomes.

PREREQUISITES AND PROBABILITIES

When there is some endeavor with five prerequisites for success, then by definition the chances of success in that endeavor depend on the chances of having all five of those prerequisites simultaneously. Even if none of these

1

prerequisites is rare— for example, if these prerequisites are all so common that chances are two out of three that any given person has any one of those five prerequisites— nevertheless the odds are against having all five of the prerequisites for success in that endeavor.

When the chances of having any one of the five prerequisites are two out of three, as in this example, the chance of having all five is two-thirds multiplied by itself five times.* That comes out to be 32/243 in this example, or about one out of eight. In other words, the chances of failure are about seven out of eight. This is obviously a very skewed distribution of success, and nothing like a normal bell curve of distribution of outcomes that we might expect otherwise.

What does this little exercise in arithmetic mean in the real world? One conclusion is that we should not expect success to be evenly or randomly distributed among individuals, groups, institutions or nations in endeavors with multiple prerequisites— which is to say, most meaningful endeavors. And if these are indeed prerequisites, then having four out of five prerequisites means nothing, as far as successful outcomes are concerned. In other words, people with most of the prerequisites for success may nevertheless be utter failures.

Whether a prerequisite that is missing is complex or simple, its absence can negate the effect of all the other prerequisites that are present. If you are illiterate, for example, all the other good qualities that you may have in abundance count for nothing in many, if not most, careers today. As late as 1950, more than 40 percent of the world's adult population were still illiterate. That included more than half the adults in Asia and Africa.[1]

If you are not prepared to undergo the extended toil and sacrifice that some particular endeavor may require, then despite having all the native potential for great success in that endeavor, and with all the doors of opportunity wide open, you can nevertheless become an utter failure.

Not all the prerequisites are necessarily within the sole control of the individual who has them or does not have them. Even extraordinary capacities in one or some of the prerequisites can mean nothing in the ultimate outcome in some endeavors.

---

* $\frac{2}{3} \times \frac{2}{3} \times \frac{2}{3} \times \frac{2}{3} \times \frac{2}{3} = \frac{32}{243}$

Back in the early twentieth century, for example, Professor Lewis M. Terman of Stanford University launched a research project that followed 1,470 people with IQs of 140 and above for more than half a century. Data on the careers of men in this group— from a time when full-time careers for women were less common[*]— showed serious disparities even within this rare group, all of whom had IQs within the top one percent.

Some of these men had highly successful careers, others had more modest achievements, and about 20 percent were clearly disappointments. Of 150 men in this less successful category, only 8 received a graduate degree, and dozens of them received only a high school diploma. A similar number of the most successful men in Terman's group received 98 graduate degrees[2]— more than a tenfold disparity among men who were all in the top one percent in IQ.

Meanwhile, two men who were tested in childhood, and who failed to make the 140 IQ cutoff level, later earned Nobel Prizes— as none of the men with IQs of 140 and above did.[3] Clearly, then, all the men in Terman's group had at least one prerequisite for that extraordinary achievement— namely, a high enough IQ. And, equally clearly, there must have been other prerequisites that hundreds of these men with IQs in the top one percent did not have.

As for factors behind differences in educational and career outcomes within Terman's group, the biggest differentiating factor was in family backgrounds. Men with the most outstanding achievements came from middle-class and upper-class families, and were raised in homes where there were many books. Half of their fathers were college graduates, at a time when that was far more rare than today.[4]

Among those men who were least successful, nearly one-third had a parent who had dropped out of school before the eighth grade.[5] Even extraordinary IQs did not eliminate the need for other prerequisites.

Sometimes what is missing may be simply someone to point an individual with great potential in the right direction. An internationally renowned scholar

---

[*] As of 1940, just under half of the women in the Terman group were employed full time. Lewis M. Terman, et al., *The Gifted Child Grows Up: Twenty-Five Years' Follow-Up of a Superior Group* (Stanford: Stanford University Press, 1947), p. 177.

once mentioned, at a social gathering, that when he was a young man he had not thought about going to college— until someone else urged him to do so. Nor was he the only person of exceptional ability of whom that was true.*

Some other people, including people without his great abilities, would automatically apply to college if they came from particular social groups where that was a norm. But without that one person who urged him to seek higher education, this particular internationally renowned scholar might well have become a fine automobile mechanic or a worker in some other manual occupation, but not a world-class scholar.

There may be more or less of an approximation of a normal bell curve, as far as how many people have any particular prerequisite, and yet a very skewed distribution of success, based on having all the prerequisites simultaneously. This is not only true in theory, empirical evidence suggests that it is true also in practice.

In golf, for example, there is something of an approximation of a bell curve when it comes to the distribution of such examples of individual skills as the number of putts per round of golf, or driving distances off the tee. And yet there is a grossly skewed distribution of outcomes requiring a whole range of golf skills— namely, winning Professional Golfers Association (PGA) tournaments.[6]

Most professional golfers have never won a single PGA tournament in their entire lives,[7] while just three golfers— Arnold Palmer, Jack Nicklaus and Tiger Woods— won more than 200 PGA tournaments between them.[8] Moreover, there are similarly skewed distributions of peak achievements in baseball and tennis, among other endeavors.[9]

Given multiple prerequisites for many human endeavors, we should not be surprised if economic or social advances are not evenly or randomly distributed among individuals, groups, institutions or nations at any given time. Nor should we be surprised if the laggards in one century forge ahead in some later century, or if world leaders in one era become laggards in

---

* Distinguished economist Richard Rosett was another example. See Thomas Sowell, *The Einstein Syndrome: Bright Children Who Talk Late* (New York: Basic Books, 2001), pp. 47–48. The best-selling author of *Hillbilly Elegy* was another. See J.D. Vance, *Hillbilly Elegy: A Memoir of a Family and Culture in Crisis* (New York: HarperCollins, 2016) pp. 2, 129–130, 205, 239.

another era. When the gain or loss of just one prerequisite can turn failure into success or turn success into failure, it should not be surprising, in a changing world, if the leaders and laggards of one century or millennium exchange places in some later century or millennium.

If the prerequisites themselves change over time, with the development of new kinds of endeavors, or if advances in human knowledge revolutionize existing endeavors, the chance of a particular pattern of success and failure becoming permanent may be greatly reduced.

Perhaps the most revolutionary change in the evolution of human societies was the development of agriculture— within the last 10 percent of the existence of the human species. Agriculture made possible the feeding of concentrated populations in cities, which in turn have been (and remain) the sources of most of the landmark scientific, technological and other advances of the human race that we call civilization.[10]

The earliest known civilizations arose in geographic settings with strikingly similar characteristics. These include river valleys subject to annual floodings, whether in ancient Mesopotamia, in the valley of the Indus River on the Indian subcontinent in ancient times, along the Nile in ancient Egypt, or in the Yellow River valley in ancient China.[11]

Clearly there were other prerequisites, since these particular combinations of things had not produced agriculture, or civilizations dependent on agriculture, for most of the existence of the human species. Genetic characteristics peculiar to the races in these particular locations hardly seem likely to be the key factor, since the populations of these areas are by no means in the forefront of human achievements today.

Patterns of very skewed distributions of success have long been common in the real world— and such skewed outcomes contradict some fundamental assumptions on both the political left and right. People on opposite sides of many issues may both assume a background level of probabilities that is not realistic.

Yet that flawed perception of probabilities— and the failure of the real world to match expectations derived from that flawed perception— can drive ideological movements, political crusades and judicial decisions, up to and including decisions by the Supreme Court of the United States, where "disparate impact" statistics, showing different outcomes for different groups, have been enough to create a presumption of discrimination.

In the past, similar statistical disparities were enough to promote genetic determinism, from which came eugenics, laws forbidding inter-racial marriages and, where there were other prerequisites for monumental catastrophe, the Holocaust.

In short, gross disparities among peoples in their economic outcomes, scientific discoveries, technological advances and other achievements have inspired efforts at explanation that span the ideological spectrum. To subject these explanations to the test of facts, it may be useful to begin by examining some empirical evidence about disparities among individuals, social groups, institutions and nations.

EMPIRICAL EVIDENCE

Behind many attempts to explain, and change, glaring disparities in outcomes among human beings is the implicit assumption that such disparities would not exist without corresponding disparities in either people's genetic makeup or in the way they are treated by other people. These disparities exist both among individuals and among aggregations of people organized into institutions of various sorts, ranging from families to businesses to whole nations.

Skewed distributions of outcomes are also common in nature, in outcomes over which humans have no control, ranging from lightning to earthquakes and tornadoes.

People
While it might seem plausible that equal, or at least comparable, outcomes would exist among people in various social groups, in the absence of some biased human intervention, or some genetic differences affecting those people's outcomes, neither belief survives the test of empirical evidence.

A study of National Merit Scholarship finalists, for example, found that, among finalists from five-child families, the first-born was the finalist more often than the other four siblings combined.[12] If there is not equality of outcomes among people born to the same parents and raised under the same roof, why should equality of outcomes be expected— or assumed— when conditions are not nearly so comparable? First-borns were also a majority of the finalists in two-child, three-child, and four-child families.[13]

Such results are a challenge to believers in either heredity or environment, as those terms are conventionally used.

IQ data from Britain, Germany and the United States showed that the average IQ of first-born children was higher than the average IQ of their later-born siblings. Moreover, the average IQ of second-born children as a group was higher than the average IQ of third-born children.[14]

A similar pattern was found among young men given mental tests for military service in the Netherlands. The first-born averaged higher mental test scores than their siblings, and the other siblings likewise averaged higher scores than those born after them.[15] Similar results were found in mental test results for Norwegians.[16] The sample sizes in these studies ranged into the hundreds of thousands.[17]

These advantages of the first-born seem to carry over into later life in many fields. Data on male medical students at the University of Michigan, class of 1968, showed that the proportion of first-born men in that class was more than double the proportion of later-born men as a group, and more than ten times the proportion among men who were fourth-born or later.[18] A 1978 study of applicants to a medical school in New Jersey showed the first-born over-represented among the applicants, and still more so among the successful applicants.[19]

Most other countries do not have as high a proportion of their young people go on to a college or university education as in the United States. But, whatever the proportion in a given country, the first-born tend to go on to higher education more often than do later siblings. A study of Britons in 2003 showed that 22 percent of those who were the eldest child went on to receive a degree, compared to 11 percent of those who were the fourth child and 3 percent of those who were the tenth child.[20]

A study of more than 20,000 young people in late twentieth-century France showed that 18 percent of those males who were an only child completed four years of college, compared to 16 percent of male first-born children— and just 7 percent of males who were fifth-born or later born. Among females the disparity was slightly larger. Twenty-three percent who were an only child completed four years of college, compared to 19 percent who were first-born, and just 5 percent of those who were fifth-born or later.[21]

Birth order differences persist as people move into their careers. A study of about 4,000 Americans concluded that "The decline in average earnings is even more pronounced" than the decline in education between those born earlier and those born later.[22] Other studies have shown the first-born to be over-represented among lawyers in the greater Boston area[23] and among Members of Congress.[24] Of the 29 original astronauts in the Apollo program that put a man on the moon, 22 were either first-born or an only child.[25] The first-born and the only child were also over-represented among leading composers of classical music.[26]

Consider how many things are the same for children born to the same parents and raised under the same roof— race, the family gene pool, economic level, cultural values, educational opportunities, parents' educational and intellectual levels, as well as the family's relatives, neighbors and friends— and yet the difference in birth order alone has made a demonstrable difference in outcomes.

Whatever the general advantages or disadvantages the children in a particular family may have, the only obvious advantage that applies only to the first-born, or to an only child, is the undivided attention of the parents during early childhood development.

The fact that twins tend to average several points lower IQs than people born singly[27] reinforces this inference. Conceivably, the lower average IQs of twins might have originated in the womb but, when one of the twins is stillborn or dies early, the surviving twin averages an IQ closer to that of people born singly.[28] This suggests that with twins, as with other children, the divided or undivided attention of the parents may be key.

In addition to quantitatively different amounts of parental attention available to children born earlier and later than their siblings, there are also qualitative differences in parental attention to children in general, from one social class to another. Children of parents with professional occupations have been found to hear 2,100 words per hour, while children from working-class families hear 1,200 words per hour, and children from families on welfare hear 600 words per hour.[29] Other studies suggest that there are also qualitative differences in the *manner* of parent-child interactions in different social classes.[30]

Against this background, expectations or assumptions of equal or comparable outcomes from children raised in such different ways have no basis. Nor can different outcomes in schools, colleges or employment be automatically attributed to those who teach, grade or hire them, when empirical evidence shows that how people were raised can affect how they turn out as adults.

It is not simply that they may have different levels of ability as adults. People from different social backgrounds may also have different goals and priorities— a possibility paid little or no attention in many studies that measure how much opportunity there is by how much upward movement takes place,[31] as if everyone is equally striving to move up.

Most notable achievements involve multiple factors— beginning with a desire to succeed in the particular endeavor, and a willingness to do what it takes, without which all the native ability in an individual and all the opportunity in a society mean nothing, just as the desire and the opportunity mean nothing without the ability.

What this suggests, among other things, is that an individual, a people, or a nation may have some, many or most of the prerequisites for a given achievement without having any real success in producing that achievement. And yet that individual, that people or that nation may suddenly burst upon the scene with spectacular success when whatever the missing factor or factors are finally get added to the mix.

Poor and backward nations that suddenly moved to the forefront of human achievements include Scotland, beginning in the eighteenth century, and Japan beginning in the nineteenth century. Both had rapid rises, as time is measured in history.

Scotland was for centuries one of the poorest, most economically and educationally lagging nations on the outer fringes of European civilization. There was said to be no fourteenth-century Scottish baron who could write his own name.[32] And yet, in the eighteenth and nineteenth centuries, a disproportionate number of the leading intellectual figures in Britain were of Scottish ancestry— including James Watt in engineering, Adam Smith in economics, David Hume in philosophy, Joseph Black in chemistry, Sir Walter Scott in literature, and James Mill and John Stuart Mill in economic and political writings.

Among the changes that had occurred among the Scots was their Protestant churches' crusade promoting the idea that everyone should learn to read, so as to be able to read the Bible personally, rather than have priests tell them what it says and means. Another change was a more secular, but still fervent, crusade to learn the English language, which replaced their native Gaelic among the Scottish lowlanders, and thereby opened up far more fields of written knowledge to the Scots.

In some of those fields, including medicine and engineering, the Scots eventually excelled the English, and became renowned internationally. These were mostly Scottish lowlanders, rather than highlanders, who continued to speak Gaelic for generations longer.

Japan was likewise a poor, poorly educated and technologically backward nation, as late as the middle of the nineteenth century. The Japanese were astonished to see a train for the first time, that train being presented to them by American Commodore Matthew Perry, whose ships visited Japan in 1853.[33] Yet, after later generations of extraordinary national efforts to catch up with the Western world technologically, these efforts led to Japan's being in the forefront of technology in a number of fields in the latter half of the twentieth century. Among other things, Japan produced a bullet train that exceeded anything produced in the United States.

Other extraordinary advances have been made by a particular people, rather than by a nation state. We have become so used to seeing numerous world-class performances by Jewish intellectual figures in the arts and sciences that it is necessary to note that this has been an achievement that burst upon the world as a widespread social phenomenon in the nineteenth and twentieth centuries, even though there had been isolated Jewish intellectual figures of international stature in some earlier centuries.

As a distinguished economic historian put it: "Despite their vast advantage in literacy and human capital for many centuries, Jews played an almost negligible role in the history of science and technology before and during the early Industrial Revolution" and "the great advances in science and mathematics between 1600 and 1750 do not include work associated with Jewish names."[34]

Whatever the potentialities of Jews during the era of the industrial revolution, and despite their literacy and other human capital, there was often little opportunity for them to gain access to the institutions of the wider society in Europe, where the industrial revolution began. Jews were not admitted to most universities in Europe prior to the nineteenth century.

Late in the eighteenth century, the United States became a pioneer in granting Jews the same legal rights as everyone else, as a result of the Constitution's general ban against federal laws that discriminate on the basis of religion. France followed suit after the revolution of 1789, and other nations began easing or eliminating various bans on Jews in various times and places during the nineteenth century.

In the wake of these developments, Jews began to flow, and then to flood, into universities. By the 1880s, for example, Jews were 30 percent of all the students at Vienna University.[35] The net result in the late nineteenth century, and in the twentieth century, was a relatively sudden proliferation of internationally renowned Jewish figures in many fields, including fields in which Jews were virtually non-existent among the leaders in earlier centuries.

From 1870 to 1950, Jews were greatly over-represented among prominent figures in the arts and sciences, relative to their proportion of the population in various European countries and in the United States. In the second half of the twentieth century, with Jews being less than one percent of the world's population, they received 22 percent of the Nobel Prizes in chemistry, 32 percent in medicine and 32 percent in physics.[36]

Here, as in other very different contexts, changes in the extent to which prerequisites are met *completely* can have dramatic effects on outcomes in a relatively short time, as history is measured. The fact that Jews rose dramatically in certain fields after various barriers were removed does not mean that other groups would do the same if barriers against them were removed, for the Jews *already* had various other prerequisites for such achievements— notably widespread literacy during centuries when illiteracy was the norm in the world at large— and Jews needed only enough additional prerequisites to complete the required ensemble.

Conversely, China was for centuries the most technologically advanced nation in the world, especially during what were called the Middle Ages in Europe. The Chinese had cast iron a thousand years before the Europeans.[37] A Chinese admiral led a voyage of discovery that was longer than Columbus' voyage, generations before Columbus' voyage,[38] and in ships far larger and technologically more advanced than Columbus' ships.[39]

One crucial decision in fifteenth-century China, however, set in motion a radical change in the relative positions of the Chinese and the Europeans. Like other nations demonstrably more advanced than others, the Chinese regarded those others as innately inferior— as "barbarians," just as the Romans likewise regarded peoples beyond the domain of the Roman Empire.

Convinced by the exploratory voyages of its ships that there was nothing to be learned from other peoples in other places, the government of China decided in 1433 to not only discontinue such voyages, but to *forbid* such voyages, or the building of ships capable of making such voyages, and to greatly reduce the influence of the outside world on Chinese society.

Plausible as this decision might have seemed at the time, it came as Europe was emerging from its "dark ages" of retrogression in the wake of the decline and fall of the Roman Empire, and was now experiencing a Renaissance of progress in many ways— including progress based on developing things that had originated in China, such as printing and gunpowder. Columbus' ships, though not up to the standards of those once made in China, were sufficient to cross the Atlantic Ocean in search of a route to India— and to inadvertently make the world-changing discovery of a whole hemisphere.

In short, Europe had expanding opportunities for progress, both within itself and in the larger world opened up to it by its expansion into the other half of the planet, at a time when China's rulers had chosen the path of isolation— not total, but substantial, isolation. The strait jacket of isolation, inflicted on many parts of the world by geographic barriers that left whole peoples and nations both poor and backward,[40] was inflicted on China by its own rulers.

The net result over the centuries that followed was that China fell behind in an era of great technological and economic progress elsewhere in the world.

In the pitiless international jungle, this meant that other countries not only surpassed China but imposed their will on a vulnerable China, which declined to the status of a Third World country, partly subordinated to other countries in various ways— including a loss of territory, as the Portuguese took over the port of Macao, the British took over the port of Hong Kong and eventually Japan seized much territory on the mainland of China.

What China lost were not the prerequisites represented by the qualities of its people, but the wisdom of its rulers who, with one crucial decision— the loss of just one prerequisite— forfeited the country's preeminence in the world.

That the qualities of the Chinese people endured was evidenced by the worldwide success of millions of "overseas Chinese" emigrants, who arrived in many countries in Southeast Asia and in the Western Hemisphere, often destitute and with little education— and yet rose over the generations to prosperity, and in many individual cases even great wealth.

The contrast between the fate of China and the fate of the "overseas Chinese" was demonstrated when, as late as 1994, the 57 million "overseas Chinese" produced as much wealth as the billion people living in China.[41]

Among the more dire national projects that failed among other nations— fortunately, in this case— for lack of one prerequisite was the attempt by Nazi Germany to create a nuclear bomb. Hitler not only had such a program, he had it before the United States launched a similar program. Germany was, at that point, in the forefront of science in nuclear physics. However, it so happened that, at that particular juncture in history, many of the leading nuclear physicists in the world were Jewish— and Hitler's fanatical anti-Semitism not only precluded their participation in his nuclear bomb project, his threat to the survival of Jews in general led many of these physicists to leave Europe and immigrate to the United States.

It was expatriate Jewish nuclear physicists who brought the threat of a Nazi nuclear bomb to President Roosevelt's attention, and urged the creation of an American program to create such a bomb before the Nazis got one. Moreover, Jewish scientists— both expatriate and American— played a major role in the development of the American nuclear bomb.[42]

These scientists were a key resource that the United States had and that Hitler could not have, as a result of his own racial fanaticism. The whole world escaped the prospect of mass annihilation and/or crushing subjugation to Nazi oppression and dehumanization because Hitler's nuclear program lacked one key factor. He had some leading nuclear physicists, but not enough.

Institutions

China was by no means the only nation to forfeit a superior position among the nations of the world. Ancient Greece and the Roman Empire were far more advanced than their British or Scandinavian contemporaries, who were largely illiterate at a time when Greeks and Romans had landmark intellectual giants, and were laying the intellectual and material foundations of Western civilization. As late as the tenth century, a Muslim scholar noted that Europeans grew more pale the farther north you go and also that the "farther they are to the north the more stupid, gross, and brutish they are."[43]

Such a correlation between complexion and ability would be taboo today, but there is little reason to doubt that a very real correlation existed among Europeans as of the time when this observation was made. The fact that Northern Europe and Western Europe would move ahead of Southern Europe economically and technologically many centuries later was a heartening sign that backwardness in a given era does not mean backwardness forever. But that does not deny that great economic and social disparities have existed among peoples and nations at given times and places.

Particular institutions, such as business enterprises, have likewise risen or fallen dramatically over time. Any number of leading American businesses today began at the level of the lowly peddler (Macy's and Bloomingdale's, for example), or were started by men born in poverty (J.C. Penney; F.W. Woolworth) or began in a garage (Hewlett Packard). Conversely, there have been leading businesses that have declined from the pinnacles of profitable success, even into bankruptcy— sometimes with the loss of just one prerequisite.

For more than a hundred years, the Eastman Kodak company was the dominant firm in the photographic industry throughout the world. It was George Eastman who, in the late nineteenth century, first made photography accessible to great numbers of ordinary people, with his cameras and film that did not require the technical expertise of professional photographers. Before Kodak cameras and film appeared, professional photographers had to know how to apply light-sensitive emulsions to photographic plates that went into big, cumbersome cameras, and know how to later chemically develop the images taken and then print pictures.

Small and simple Kodak cameras, and rolls of Kodak film in place of photographic plates, enabled people with no technical knowledge at all to take pictures and then leave the developing and printing of those pictures to others.

Kodak cameras and film spread internationally. For decades, Eastman Kodak sold most of the film in the entire world. It continued to sell most of the film in the world market, even after film began to be produced in other countries and Fuji film from Japan made major inroads in the late twentieth century, gaining a 21 percent market share by 1993.[44] Eastman Kodak also supplied both amateur and professional photographers with a wide range of photographic equipment and supplies, based on film technology.

For more than a century, Eastman Kodak clearly had all the prerequisites for success. As of 1988, the company employed more than 145,000 workers around the world, and its annual revenues peaked at nearly $16 billion in 1996.[45] Yet its worldwide dominance came to a remarkably sudden end in the early twenty-first century, when its income plummeted and the company collapsed into bankruptcy.[46]

Just one key factor changed in the photographic industry— the substitution of digital cameras for film cameras. Worldwide sales of film cameras peaked in the year 2000, when those sales were more than four times the sales of digital cameras. But, three years later, digital camera sales in 2003 surpassed film camera sales for the first time. Then, just two years later, digital camera sales exceeded the peak sales that film cameras had reached in 2000, and now digital camera sales were more than four times the sales of film cameras.[47]

Eastman Kodak, which had produced the world's first electronic image sensor,[48] was undone by its own invention, which other companies developed to higher levels in digital cameras. These included electronics companies not initially in the photographic industry, such as Sony, whose share of the digital camera market was more than double that of Eastman Kodak by the end of the twentieth century and in the early twenty-first century,[49] when digital camera sales skyrocketed.

With the sudden collapse of the market for film cameras, Kodak's vast array of photographic apparatus and supplies, based on film technology, suddenly lost most of their market, and the Eastman Kodak company disintegrated economically. Its mastery of existing prerequisites for success meant nothing when just one of those prerequisites changed. Nor was this descent from industrial world dominance to bankruptcy unique to Eastman Kodak.*

Nature

In nature, as in human endeavors, there can be multiple prerequisites for various natural phenomena, and these multiple prerequisites can likewise lead to very skewed distributions of outcomes.

---

* More than half a century before the collapse of Eastman Kodak, economist J.A. Schumpeter pointed out that the most powerful economic competition is not that between producers of the same product, as so often assumed, but the competition between old and new technologies and methods of organization. In the case of Eastman Kodak, it was not the competition of Fuji film, but the competition of digital cameras, that was decisive. For Schumpeter, it was not the competition of firms producing the same products, as in economics textbooks, that was decisive. In Schumpeter's words, "it is not that kind of competition which counts but the competition from the new commodity, the new technology, the new source of supply, the new type of organization (the largest-scale unit of control, for instance)— competition which commands a decisive cost or quality advantage and which strikes not at the margins of the profits and the outputs of the existing firms but at their foundations and their very lives." Joseph A. Schumpeter, *Capitalism, Socialism, and Democracy*, third edition (New York: Harper & Brothers, 1950), p. 84.

While some have found it surprising that genetic similarities between chimpanzees and human beings extend to well over 90 percent of their genetic makeup, what may be more surprising is that even a microscopic, worm-like creature also has most of its genetic makeup match that of human beings.[50] But having many or most prerequisites can count for nothing as far as producing the ultimate outcome.

Multiple factors have to come together in order to create tornadoes, and more than 90 percent of all the tornadoes in the entire world occur in just one country— the United States.[51] Yet there is nothing startlingly unique about either the climate or the terrain of the United States that cannot be found, as individual features, in various other places around the world. But all the prerequisites for tornadoes do not come together as often in the rest of the world as in the United States.

Similarly, lightning occurs more often in Africa than in Europe and Asia put together, even though Asia alone is larger than Africa or any other continent.[52] Among many other skewed distributions in nature is the fact that earthquakes are as common around the rim of the Pacific Ocean, both in Asia and in the Western Hemisphere, as they are rare around the rim of the Atlantic.[53]

Among other highly skewed outcomes in nature is that some geographic settings produce many times more species than others. The Amazon region of South America is one such setting:

> South America's Amazon Basin contains the world's largest expanse of tropical rainforest. Its diversity is renowned. On a single Peruvian tree, Wilson (1988) found 43 species of ants, comparable to the entire ant fauna of the British Isles.[54]

Similar gross disparities have also been found between the number of species of fish in the Amazon region of South America, compared to the number in Europe: "Eight times as many species of fish have been caught in an Amazonian pond the size of a tennis court as exist in all the rivers of Europe."[55]

IMPLICATIONS

What can we conclude from all these examples of highly skewed distributions of outcomes around the world? Neither in nature nor among human beings are either equal or randomly distributed outcomes automatic. On the contrary, grossly unequal distributions of outcomes are common, both in nature and among people, in circumstances where neither genes nor discrimination are involved.

What seems a more tenable conclusion is that, as economic historian David S. Landes put it, "The world has never been a level playing field."[56] The idea that it *would* be a level playing field, if it were not for either genes or discrimination, is a preconception in defiance of both logic and facts. Nothing is easier to find than sins among human beings, but to automatically make those sins the sole, or even primary, cause of different outcomes among different peoples is to ignore many other reasons for those disparities.

Geographic differences are one among other factors that make for a skewed distribution of outcomes. Coastal peoples have long tended to be more prosperous and more advanced than people of the same race living farther inland, while people living in river valleys have likewise tended to be more prosperous and more advanced than people living up in the mountains.[57]

Most of the most fertile land in the world is in the temperate zones and little or none in the tropics.[58] Areas that are both near the sea and in the temperate zones have 8 percent of the world's inhabited land area, 23 percent of the world's population, and 53 percent of the world's Gross Domestic Product.[59]

Neither genetics nor discrimination is either necessary or sufficient to account for such skewed outcomes. This does not mean that either genes or discrimination can simply be dismissed as a possibility in any given circumstance, but only that hard evidence would be required to substantiate either of these possibilities, which remain testable hypotheses, without being foregone conclusions.

Given how widely, how long and how strongly each of these two explanations— that is, genes or discrimination— has dominated thinking, laws and policies in various parts of the world, it is no small matter to escape from having painted ourselves into a corner with either of these sweeping preconceptions.

Two of the monumental catastrophes of the twentieth century— Nazism and Communism— led to the slaughter of millions of human beings, in the name of either ridding the world of the burden of "inferior" races or ridding the world of "exploiters" responsible for the poverty of the exploited. While each of these beliefs might have been testable hypotheses, their greatest political triumphs came as dogmas placed beyond the reach of evidence or logic.

Neither Hitler's *Mein Kampf* nor Marx's *Capital* was an exercise in hypothesis testing. While Karl Marx's vast three-volume economic treatise was a far greater intellectual achievement, "exploitation" was at no point in its 2,500 pages treated as a testable hypothesis, but was instead the foundation assumption on which an elaborate intellectual superstructure was built. And that proved to be a foundation of quicksand. Getting rid of capitalist "exploiters" in Communist countries did not raise the living standards of workers, even to levels common in many capitalist countries, where workers were presumably still being exploited, as Marxists conceived the term.

Discrimination as an explanation of economic and social disparities may have a similar emotional appeal for many. But we can at least try to treat these, and alternative theories, as testable hypotheses. The historic consequences of treating beliefs as sacred dogmas beyond the reach of evidence or logic should be enough to dissuade us from going down that road again, despite how exciting or emotionally satisfying political dogmas and the crusades resulting from those dogmas can be, or how convenient in sparing us the drudgery and discomfort of having to think through our own beliefs or test them against facts.

Chapter 2

DISCRIMINATION:

MEANINGS and COSTS

Some people are said to have discriminating tastes when they are especially discerning in detecting differences in qualities and choosing accordingly, whether choosing wines, paintings or other goods and services. But the word is also used in an almost opposite sense to refer to arbitrary differences in behavior toward people, based on their group identities, regardless of their actual qualities as individuals.

Both kinds of discrimination can result in large differences in outcomes, whether judging people or things. Wine connoisseurs can end up choosing one kind of wine far more often than another, and paying far more for a bottle of one kind of wine than for a bottle of the other.

Something similar can often be observed when it comes to people. It is common, in countries around the world, for some groups to have very different outcomes when they are judged by others in employment, educational and other contexts. Thus different groups may end up with very different incomes, occupations and unemployment rates, or very different rates of admissions to colleges and universities, among many other group disparities in outcomes.

The fundamental question is: Which kind of discrimination has led to such disparate outcomes? Have differences in qualities between individuals or groups been correctly discerned by others or have those others made their decisions based on personal aversions or arbitrary assumptions about members of particular groups? This is ultimately an empirical question, even if attempts to answer that question evoke passionate feelings and passionate certainty by observers reaching opposite conclusions.

Another way of saying the same thing is: Are group disparities in outcomes a result of *internal* differences in behavior and capabilities, accurately assessed by outsiders, or are those disparities due to *external* impositions based on the biased misjudgments or antagonisms of outsiders?

The answers to such questions are not necessarily the same for all group disparities, nor necessarily the same for a given group at different times and places. Seeking the answers to such questions is more than an academic exercise, when the ultimate purpose is to enable more fellow human beings to have better prospects of advancing themselves. But, before seeking answers, we need to be very clear about the words we use in asking the question.

MEANINGS OF DISCRIMINATION

At a minimum, we need to know what we ourselves mean when we use a word like "discrimination," especially since it has conflicting meanings. The broader meaning— an ability to discern differences in the qualities of people and things, and choosing accordingly— can be called Discrimination I, making fact-based distinctions. The narrower, but more commonly used, meaning— treating people negatively, based on arbitrary assumptions or aversions concerning individuals of a particular race or sex, for example— can be called Discrimination II, the kind of discrimination that has led to anti-discrimination laws and policies.

Ideally, Discrimination I, applied to people, would mean judging each person as an individual, regardless of what group that person is part of. But here, as in other contexts, the ideal is seldom found among human beings in the real world, even among people who espouse that ideal.

If you are walking at night down a lonely street, and see up ahead a shadowy figure in an alley, do you judge that person as an individual or do you cross the street and pass on the other side? The shadowy figure in the alley could turn out to be a kindly neighbor, out walking his dog. But, when making such decisions, a mistake on your part could be costly, up to and including costing you your life.

In other contexts, you may in fact judge each person as an individual. But that this depends on context means that people have already been implicitly pre-sorted by the context, and only after that pre-sorting are they then judged as individuals. For example, a professor entering a classroom on the first day of the academic year may judge and treat each student as an individual. But that same professor, walking down a lonely street at night, may not judge and react to each stranger on the road ahead as an individual.

The students in a college classroom are not likely to be a random sample of the full range of variations found in the general population, and are more likely to represent a narrower range of people assembled there for a narrower range of purposes, and with a narrower range of individual characteristics, as well as being in a setting less dangerous than a dark street at night.

In short, one of the differences between the applicability of Discrimination I and Discrimination II is cost— and this is not always a small cost, nor a cost measured solely in money. Everyone might agree that Discrimination I is preferable, other things being equal, because it means making decisions based on demonstrable realities. Nevertheless, one may still be aware that other things are not always equal, and sometimes other things are very far from being equal.

Where there is a difference in costs when choosing between Discrimination I and Discrimination II, much may depend on how high those costs are, and especially on who pays those costs. People who would never walk through a particular neighborhood at night, or perhaps not even in broad daylight, may nevertheless be indignant at banks that engage in "redlining"— that is, putting a whole neighborhood off-limits as a place to invest their depositors' money. The observers' own "redlining" in their choices of where to walk may never be seen by them as a different example of the same principle.

In short, Discrimination I can have prohibitive costs in some situations, especially when it is applied at the individual level. However, Discrimination II— the arbitrary or antipathy-based bias against a group, is not the only other option. Another way of making decisions is by weighing empirical evidence about groups as a whole, or about the interactions of different groups with one another.

This is still Discrimination I, basing decisions on empirical evidence. But the distinction between the ideal version of Discrimination I—judging each individual as an individual— and making decisions based on empirical evidence about the group to which the individual belongs is a consequential difference. We can call the ideal version (basing decisions on evidence about individuals) Discrimination Ia, and the less than ideal version (basing individual decisions on group evidence) Discrimination Ib. But both are different from Discrimination II, making decisions based on unsubstantiated notions or animosities.

To take an extreme example of Discrimination Ib, for the sake of illustration, if 40 percent of the people in Group X are alcoholics and 1 percent of the people in Group Y are alcoholics, an employer may well prefer to hire only people from Group Y for work where an alcoholic would be not only ineffective but dangerous. This would mean that a majority of the people in Group X— 60 percent in this case— would be denied employment, even though they are not alcoholics.

What matters, crucially, to the employer is the *cost* of determining which individual is or is not an alcoholic, when job applicants all show up sober on the day when they are seeking employment.

This also matters to the customers who buy the employer's products and to society as a whole. If alcoholics produce a higher proportion of products that turn out to be defective, that is a cost to customers, and that cost may take different forms. For example, the customer could buy the product and then discover that it is defective. Alternatively, defects in the product might be discovered at the factory and discarded. In this case, the customers will be charged higher prices for the products that are sold, since the costs of defective products that are discovered and discarded at the factory must be covered by the prices charged for the reliable products that pass the screening test and are sold.

To the extent that alcoholics are not only less competent but dangerous, the costs of those dangers are paid by either fellow employees who face those dangers on the job or by customers who buy dangerously defective products, or both. In short, there are serious costs inherent in the situation, so that either 60 percent of the people in Group X or employers or customers— or all three groups— end up paying the costs of the alcoholism of 40 percent of the people in Group X.

This is certainly not judging each job applicant as an individual, so it is not Discrimination I in the purest sense of Discrimination Ia. On the other hand, it is also not Discrimination II, in the sense of decisions based on a personal bias or antipathy toward that group. The employer might well have personal friends from Group X, based on far more knowledge of those particular individuals than it is possible to get about job applicants, without prohibitive costs.

The point here is neither to justify nor condemn the employer but to *classify* different decision-making processes, so that their implications and consequences can be analyzed separately. If judging each person as an individual is Discrimination Ia, we can classify as Discrimination Ib basing decisions about groups on information that is correct for that group, though not necessarily correct for every individual in that group, nor necessarily even correct for a majority of the individuals in that group.

A real-life example of the effect of the cost of knowledge in this context is a study which showed that, despite the reluctance of many employers to hire young black males, because a significant proportion of them have criminal records (Discrimination Ib), those particular employers who automatically did criminal background checks on **all** their employees (Discrimination Ia) tended to hire more young black males than did other employers.[1]

In other words, where the nature of the work made criminal background checks worth the cost for all employees, it was no longer necessary to use group information to assess whether individual young black job applicants had a criminal background. This made young black job applicants without a criminal background more employable than before.

More is involved here than simply a question of nomenclature. It has implications for practical policies in the real world. Many observers, hoping to help young black males have more employment opportunities, have advocated *prohibiting* employers from asking job applicants questions about a criminal record. Moreover, the U.S. Equal Employment Opportunity Commission has sued employers who do criminal background checks on job applicants, on grounds that this was racial discrimination, even when it was applied to all job applicants, regardless of race.[2] Empirically, however, criminal background checks provided *more* employment opportunities for young black males.

In a very different situation, even employers who have no animosity or aversions against particular groups may nevertheless engage in Discrimination Ib— empirically based generalizations— when the employer knows that various groups react differently in the presence of some other group or groups.

Back in nineteenth-century America, for example, when there were many immigrants from Europe in the workforce, some groups brought their mutual antagonisms in Europe with them to America. To have a workforce including both Irish Protestants and Irish Catholics working together at that time was to risk distracting frictions and even violence, with negative effects on productivity. In other words, a workforce consisting exclusively of either group might be more efficient than a workforce consisting of both.

The same principle applies where different groups have especially positive reactions to one another. For example, the employer may be indifferent as to whether the work to be done is done by men or by women, and yet be well aware that men and women are not indifferent to each other, or else the human race would have become extinct long ago.

Therefore, in the interests of workforce efficiency, when a particular occupation is overwhelmingly chosen by women, such as nursing, the employer may be reluctant to hire a male nurse, regardless of that male nurse's individual qualifications. Conversely, where lumberjacks are overwhelmingly male, the employer may be reluctant to hire a female lumberjack, even if she is demonstrably as fully qualified as the men.

Observers who point out that particular individuals are equally qualified, regardless of sex, miss the point. An equally qualified individual may do the work just as well as others, but if some of the others are distracted from their work, the net effect can be a less efficient workforce. That is the empirical basis that can lead employers to practice Discrimination Ib in such situations, even if the employers have no bias or aversion to those less likely to be hired.

Misdiagnosing the basis for discrimination produces more than a difference in words. It can produce policies less likely to achieve their goals, or even policies that make matters worse, as in the case of forbidding employers from checking criminal records of job applicants. Moreover, higher costs are not just a problem limited to employers. Others are going to have to pay the higher costs that initially fall on employers, if those employers are to stay in business and continue to provide jobs. Many people do not like to hear economists say that there is no free lunch, but that does not change the reality.

Employment decisions are not the only decisions affected by discrimination of one sort or another.

Where there are real differences between groups, with potentially dire consequences, such as murder rates several times higher in one group than in another, Discrimination Ib may be carried to the point of "redlining" a whole neighborhood or group, even when a majority of the group avoided are not guilty of the behavior feared.

Even in a high-crime neighborhood, for example, most people are not necessarily criminals.* But the costs of sorting the local population individually can be prohibitively high. Therefore decisions are likely to be made through a cruder decision-making process, relying on empirically based generalizations— Discrimination Ib— rather than the more discerning, but costly, Discrimination Ia or an antipathy-based or bias-based Discrimination II.

One of the consequences of such situations is that a law-abiding majority in a high-crime neighborhood can end up paying a high price for the presence of a criminal minority living in their midst. Some businesses will not deliver their products— whether pizzas or furniture— to high-crime

---

* As a personal note, some years ago an elderly relative was crossing a busy thoroughfare alone in the Bronx, when she lost consciousness and fell to the ground in a high-crime neighborhood. People on the sidewalk rushed out into the street, to direct traffic around her. One of the women in the group took charge of her purse and returned it after my unconscious relative revived. Not a cent was missing from the purse.

neighborhoods, rather than risk bodily harm, including death, to their drivers.

Taxi drivers may avoid taking passengers to such neighborhoods for the same reason, even when these are black taxi drivers refusing to go into black high-crime neighborhoods, especially at night. Supermarket chains and other businesses often avoid locating local stores in such neighborhoods, for similar reasons.

All this hurts law-abiding people in high-crime neighborhoods, who are, in effect, paying a price for what other people are doing. In addition to being the principal victims of criminals in their midst, they also literally pay a price in hard cash for the behavior of others, in the higher prices usually charged for goods sold in neighborhoods where there are higher costs of doing business, due to higher levels of shoplifting, vandalism, burglary, pilferage and robbery— and higher business insurance premiums because of these and other neighborhood disorders.[3]

A study titled *The Poor Pay More* saw the poor in general as "exploited consumers,"[4] taken advantage of by stores located in low-income neighborhoods. This view was echoed in the media, in government and in academic publications.[5] Yet, because many low-income neighborhoods are also high-crime neighborhoods, *The Poor Pay More* committed an all too common error in assuming that the *cause* of some undesirable outcome can be determined by where the statistical data were collected.

In this case, researchers collected price data in the neighborhood stores. But the *causes* of those high prices were not the people who posted those prices in the stores. Moreover, while prices were higher in inner-city, low-income neighborhood stores, rates of profit on investments in such stores were *not* higher than average but *lower* than average,[6] despite some people who assumed that profit rates had to be higher, because of the higher prices.[7]

For people unaware of the economics of the situation, the higher prices may be seen as simply "price gouging" by "greedy" store owners— Discrimination II against minority neighborhoods— and a problem that the government could solve by imposing price controls, for example— as a Harlem newspaper suggested, during the 1960s furor over revelations that "the poor pay more."[8]

If, however, businesses in these neighborhoods do not recover their higher costs of doing business there in the prices they charge, they face the prospect of being forced out of business by losses. There is often a dearth of businesses in low-income, high-crime neighborhoods, which would hardly be the case if there were higher rates of profit being made from the higher prices charged in such neighborhoods.

It may be no consolation to those law-abiding citizens in a high-crime neighborhood that the higher prices they have to pay are reimbursing higher costs of doing business where they live. Meanwhile, politicians and local activists have every incentive to claim that the higher prices are due to discrimination, in the sense of Discrimination II, even when in fact the community is simply paying additional costs generated by some residents in that community.

Those local residents who created none of those costs may be victims of those who did, rather than being victims of those who charged the resulting higher prices. This is not just an abstract philosophical point or a matter of semantics. The difference between understanding the source of the higher prices and mistakenly blaming those who charged those prices— which is especially likely when most of the local businesses are owned by people who are ethnically different from the people living in the neighborhood— is the difference between doing things to lessen the problem and doing things likely to make the problem worse by driving more much-needed businesses out of the neighborhood.

Although higher prices in low-income neighborhoods are often discussed in the context of racial or ethnic minorities, the same economic consequences have been found where the people in the low-income neighborhoods are white. As the *Cincinnati Enquirer* reported: "Residents of eastern Kentucky refer to the higher prices and interest rates common in their area as the 'hillbilly tax.'"[9]

Among the things that might be done to reduce the burden of unfairness to law-abiding residents of high-crime neighborhoods could be stronger law enforcement by the police and the courts. But, to the extent that the public— both inside and outside the affected communities— sees the high prices as Discrimination II against the affected community as a whole, due to bias or antipathy by the larger society, the imposition of stronger law enforcement could be seen as just another imposition of injustice on the affected communities.

In short, whether people believe that higher prices in low-income, high-crime neighborhoods are due to Discrimination II, or to empirically-based decisions (Discrimination I), matters in terms of which policies to reduce the unfair burdens on law-abiding residents are politically feasible. Community or ethnic solidarity can be a major obstacle to seeing, believing or responding to the facts.

SIDEBAR: FACTORS BEHIND PRICE DIFFERENCES

Crime is not the only reason why prices are higher in many low-income neighborhoods. To someone unfamiliar with economics, it may seem strange that a store in a low-income neighborhood can be struggling to survive, while selling a product for a dollar that Walmart is getting rich selling for 75 cents. But the costs of running a business are among the many things that are neither equal nor random. Walmart's costs are lower in many ways, of which safer locations are just one.

Even if a local store charging a dollar is making 15 cents gross profit per item, while Walmart is making only 10 cents, if Walmart's inventory turnover rate is three times as high, then in a given time period Walmart is making 30 cents selling that item, while the local store is making 15 cents. Walmart's inventory turnover rate is in fact higher than that of even some other big box chain stores, and much higher than that of a local neighborhood store, where the same item may sit on the shelf much longer before being sold.

Delivery costs are also likely to be lower per item delivered to a Walmart store. For example, the cost of delivering 100 boxes of cereal to one giant Walmart store may be far lower than the cost of delivering ten boxes of cereal to each of ten different neighborhood stores scattered around the city. It is a hundred boxes of cereal in either case, but the cost of delivering them can be very different.

None of this tells us how much Discrimination I or Discrimination II exists in a given society— or how many disparities in outcomes are due to some other circumstances or some other decision-making process.

In some situations, there may clearly be costs deliberately imposed on a group by outsiders— Discrimination II— such as denying black American citizens the right to vote in many Southern states in times past. The racial segregation laws in those states, forcing black passengers to sit in the back of buses and trolleys, and denying them admissions to those state universities set aside for whites only, were obvious examples of clearly racial discrimination.

The original ghettos in centuries past, which forced Jews to live in a confined area and banned them from most European universities, were other examples of the same Discrimination II. Innumerable other groups in countries around the world— the "untouchables" in India being a classic example— faced even more and worse restrictions and oppressions.

These are all costs imposed by Discrimination II, and paid for by its victims. What also warrants analysis, in order to understand cause and effect, are the costs paid *by the discriminators*, because these costs are factors in how much Discrimination II can persist in particular circumstances and institutions. Such costs have no such moral, political or ideological attraction as the costs paid by victims, but the costs that discriminators have to pay, and the circumstances in which they do or do not have to pay those costs, can affect how much Discrimination II is in fact likely to be inflicted.

Understanding the costs paid by discriminators also presents opportunities for policies that can ensure that these costs cannot be evaded, as well as warnings that other policies may inadvertently free discriminators from these costs, if the circumstances are not understood.

COSTS OF DISCRIMINATION

Neither the amount nor the severity of Discrimination II is fixed permanently. It varies greatly from country to country and from one era to another in the same country. There was an era in which many American employers' advertisements for some jobs said, "No Irish Need Apply" or

"Whites Only." There was a time when some shops in Harlem, back when that was an upscale white community, had signs that read, "No Jews, and No Dogs."[10]

Nor were Americans unique. In many other places and times around the world, group discrimination— that is, Discrimination II— was so pervasive and so widely understood that no such signs were necessary. For a woman, a Jew or members of some other gro··· ·· apply for certain jobs would have been considered a presumptuous waste of the employer's time.

Discrimination II in hiring and promotions raises questions about both causation and morality. Both kinds of questions deserve to be examined— sep····ly.

Causation

In trying to understand the causes and the consequences of discrimination in hiring and promotions, it is necessary to again consider whether this is Discrimination I or Discrimination II. This is not always an easy question to answer, and in fact easy answers such as automatically equating statistical disparities in outcomes with Discrimination II can be a major obstacle to getting at the truth.

An employer who judges each job applicant individually, without regard to the applicant's group membership, can nevertheless end up with employees whose demographic makeup is very different from the demographic makeup of the local population.

One major demographic fact that is often overlooked by those who automatically equate statistical disparities in outcomes with Discrimination II is that different ethnic groups have very different median ages. Japanese Americans, for example, have a median age more than *two decades* older than the median age of Mexican Americans.[11] Even if every individual of the same age had the same income, regardless of which group that individual was part of, nevertheless there would still be serious disparities in income between Japanese Americans and Mexican Americans— as well as between many other groups.

A group with a median age in their twenties will obviously not have nearly as large a proportion of their population with 20 years of work experience as a group whose median age is in their forties. One group may therefore have a disproportionate number of people in high level occupations requiring long years of experience, while the other group may be similarly over-represented in entry-level jobs, in sports or in violent crimes, which are all activities disproportionately engaged in by the young.

Such disparities in outcomes are not automatically evidence of either outsiders' biases or internal deficiencies in the groups. Either or both may be present or absent, but that requires specific empirical evidence going beyond gross statistical differences in outcomes.

In short, conditions *prior* to job applicants' reaching an employer can have a "disparate impact" on the chances of someone from a particular group being hired or promoted, even if the employer judges each applicant on that applicant's own individual qualifications, without regard to the group from which the applicant came.

Age is just one of those pre-existing conditions. As already noted, children raised in families where the parents have professional occupations hear nearly twice as many words per hour as children raised in working-class families, and more than three times as many words per hour as children raised in families on welfare.[12]

Can we believe that such differences— and others— compounded over many years while growing up, make no difference in individual abilities and social outcomes when those children become adults seeking employment? All these individuals may have been very similar at birth, but many things happen between birth and applying for a job or for college admissions. And it seldom happens the same for everybody. As we have seen, it happens differently for children born and raised in the same family, who happen to have been born earlier or later.

Not only differences in child-rearing, but also decisions made by individuals themselves, affect their outcomes. When more than three-quarters of all college degrees in education go to women and more than three-quarters of all college degrees in engineering go to men,[13] the statistical predominance of women in teaching and men in engineering cannot automatically be attributed to employers' biases.

More fundamentally, the cause of a given outcome is an empirical question, whose answer requires untangling many complex factors, rather than simply pointing dramatically and indignantly to statistical disparities in outcomes, as so often happens in politics and in the media.

Costs and Their Effects

It is easy to understand how being denied an opportunity to be hired or promoted for some jobs can lead to some groups' having lower incomes than others, and why that can arouse moral objections, not only from those denied jobs but also from others who find such practices morally repugnant.

From a causal perspective, other questions arise as to the reasons for such practices. Here the cost of discrimination *to the discriminator* plays a causal role in the outcome. There is also a cost for society at large. A society in which women are arbitrarily banned from many kinds of work can pay a huge cost by forfeiting the productive potential of half its population.

"Society," however, is seldom a decision-making unit, except perhaps at election time or during a mass uprising. To understand decisions in general, or employment decisions in particular, requires understanding the incentives and constraints confronting the particular decision-makers in particular kinds of institutions, who cannot simply choose to do whatever they wish, without regard to the costs of their decisions to themselves.

In a competitive market for labor, or for the sale of the employers' products, the validity of the beliefs behind a business owner's decisions can determine whether that business operates at a profit or a loss, and whether it survives or is forced to go out of business. In short, we cannot simply go directly from attitudes to outcomes— even if these attitudes involve racism or sexism— as if there were no intermediate factor of *costs* for decisions made in a competitive market. A systemic analysis of markets cannot proceed as if there were no other factors involved besides what individual decision-makers happen to prefer.

Economists who have recognized this have ranged from followers of Adam Smith to followers of Karl Marx. The point was perhaps best expressed by Friedrich Engels, co-author with Marx of *The Communist Manifesto*. Engels said: "what each individual wills is obstructed by everyone else, and what emerges is something that no one willed."[14] An analysis of systemic causation is concerned with what emerges.

Adam Smith, patron saint of free-market capitalism, likewise had a systemic analysis of causation. He did not attribute the benefits of a capitalist economy to good intentions by capitalists.[15] On the contrary, a case could be made that Adam Smith's view of capitalists as individuals was even more negative than that of Karl Marx.[16] Smith and Marx reached opposite conclusions as to the benefits or harm done by free-market capitalism, but neither based his conclusions on the intentions of capitalists. Each based his conclusions on the systemic incentives and constraints of economic competition.

Too many other observers, including some academic scholars, reason as if intentions automatically translate directly into outcomes. Thus, in his book *The Declining Significance of Race*, sociologist William Julius Wilson pointed out the various organized ways in which white Southern landowners and employers in the post-Civil-War South sought to keep down the earnings of black workers and black sharecroppers.[17] But there was no reference in that book to empirical evidence on how those intentions actually turned out— in other words, on "what emerges," as Engels put it.

By contrast, economist Robert Higgs, who researched the actual consequences of those efforts of white employers and landowners in the postbellum South, found that such organized efforts often collapsed, as a result of competition among white employers and landowners for black workers and sharecroppers.[18] It might seem as if newly freed blacks— desperately poor, often illiterate and unfamiliar with working as free people in labor markets— would be easy prey for whites united to enforce whatever wage and sharecropper conditions they wanted. But to expect such opportunities to prevail continuously ignores the inherent, systemic competitive pressures in a market economy.

In agriculture, especially— and the South was largely agricultural at the time— there is an inherent urgency about getting the land plowed and the seeds planted in the spring, or else there will be no crop in the fall. Those white landowners who were the first to violate the terms to which other white landowners sought to limit the economic benefits to black workers and sharecroppers stood to be the first to assure themselves of a workforce sufficient in both quantity and quality to maximize the size of the crop that could be grown on a given piece of land.

Other white landowners, who stuck by the restrictions and/or who cheated the black workers and sharecroppers in various ways, tended to find themselves having to make do with whatever quantity and quality of black workers and sharecroppers remained, after other white landowners had skimmed the cream by paying higher wages and higher crop shares to improve their own prospects of a profitable crop.

It is hardly surprising that organized efforts at suppressing black workers' pay and black sharecroppers' shares of their crops often broke down under such economic pressures. "What emerges" in this case was that black incomes per capita in 1900 were, at a minimum, "almost half again" higher than they had been in 1867–68. This represented a rate of growth higher than that in the American economy as a whole during that period.[19] Because they started from a far lower economic level, blacks were still poorer than whites. But Professor Higgs' data indicated that "black incomes grew more rapidly than white incomes over the last third of the nineteenth century."[20] And about ninety percent of blacks lived in the South during that era.

Businesses in general, whether making decisions in a labor market or a product market, are not like professors voting at a faculty meeting, because those votes seldom have any costs for the professors themselves, despite whatever good or bad results such votes may have for students or for the academic institution. The difference is the difference between decisions made subject to consequential feedback in a competitive market and decisions made with insulation from such feedback in academia and other insulated venues.

South Africa Under Apartheid

To avoid endless and inconclusive debates about the presence or magnitude of racism, we can test our hypotheses about the costs of discrimination in a context where there is no ambiguity on the subject—namely, South Africa during the era of apartheid, ruled by a white minority government, elected with the black majority denied a vote, and openly promoting white supremacy.

Apartheid laws limited how many blacks could be employed in particular industries and occupations, and forbad their being hired for work above certain levels in those industries and occupations. Yet white South African employers *in competitive industries* often hired more blacks than they were allowed to under the apartheid laws, and in higher occupations than those laws permitted.

A government crackdown during the 1970s led to hundreds of firms in South Africa's construction industry being fined for violating those laws. Nor was the construction industry the only one in which competitive businesses were fined for hiring more blacks, and in higher occupations than allowed under the law. In some other industries, blacks even outnumbered whites in some particular job categories where it was illegal for blacks to be hired at all.[21]

There is no compelling evidence that the white employers violating those laws had different racial views than the white legislators who passed such laws. What was different was that employers who failed to hire black workers whom it was profitable to hire paid a price for Discrimination II, in the form of lost opportunities to make money, while the legislators who passed laws imposing Discrimination II paid no price at all. Indeed, legislators who failed to pass such laws would pay a price politically, in a situation where only whites could vote, and where white workers wanted protection from the competition of black workers.

Both the employers and the legislators were rationally pursuing their own self-interests. It was just that the institutional incentives and constraints were different in a competitive market from the incentives and constraints in a political institution. Nor were labor markets the only markets affected by the costs confronting discriminators in South Africa.

Apartheid laws made it illegal for non-whites to live in certain areas set aside by law for whites only. Yet many non-whites in fact lived in those whites-only areas. These included black American economist Walter E. Williams during a three month stay in South Africa, doing research.[22] There was at least one whites-only area in South Africa where non-whites were a majority of the residents.[23]

Here again, costs are the key. The costs to those owners of rental property in whites-only areas, who forfeited economic benefits available by refusing to rent to non-whites, competed with the costs of disobeying apartheid laws, and the latter did not always prevail.

While racists, by definition, prefer their own race to other races, individual racists, like other people, tend to prefer themselves most of all. That is what led to widespread violations of apartheid laws by white employers and landlords in competitive industries in South Africa. It cost nothing for white South Africans to vote for candidates promoting white supremacy. But the costs of refusing to hire black workers who would make their own business profitable could be considerable. Moreover, the cost of refusing to hire blacks when other businesses competing in the product market were hiring them, risked having competitors with lower prices be a threat to the survival of a business operating in a competitive market.

This is not to say that discriminatory laws and policies have no effect. There are costs to disobeying laws, as well as countervailing costs to following such laws, so outcomes depend on particular circumstances in particular times and places.

The costs of Discrimination II can be far lower, or even non-existent, in situations where free market competition does not exist, such as in (1) public utility monopolies whose prices and profit rates are directly controlled by government, (2) non-profit organizations, and of course (3) government employment. In all these particular situations, Discrimination II has tended to be far more common than in competitive markets, not only in South Africa under apartheid, but also in other countries around the world.[24]

Unless one believes that decision-makers in these particular institutions have different racial or other views than decision-makers in competitive markets, and that such differences persist over time, as new generations of decision-makers come and go, the reasons for such *institutional* differences must be sought in particular incentives and constraints growing out of differences in the circumstances of those institutions.

Institutional Incentives and Constraints

One of the landmark struggles in the civil rights movement in mid-twentieth-century America was a campaign against laws in most Southern states mandating that black passengers sit or stand only in the back of buses, with the seats up front being reserved for whites. Although many people on both sides of this struggle regarded those laws as though they had existed from time immemorial, they had not. The history of such laws illustrates again the different roles of economic incentives and constraints versus political incentives and constraints.

Three decades after the end of slavery, laws mandating racially segregated seating in municipal transit vehicles *began* to be passed in many Southern communities, toward the end of the nineteenth century. The political situation had changed from that in the period immediately after the Civil War, when U.S. troops were stationed in Southern states, and Southern governments were subject to federal policies granting blacks the right to vote during what was called the Reconstruction era.

With the end of Reconstruction, and the return of local self-government in the South, blacks often lost the right to vote, by methods ranging from laws to organized terrorism. Racially segregated seating on municipal transit vehicles was just one of the political consequences. Before these laws were passed, it was common for blacks and whites to sit wherever they felt like sitting on public transportation vehicles in the South.

Many, if not most, of the bus and trolley companies during that era were privately owned, and their profits depended on how many people— whether black or white— chose to ride in their vehicles.

The decision-makers in these privately owned companies understood that they could lose profits if offending black customers by making them sit in the back, or to stand when all the back seats were taken, even if there were vacant seats in the front section that was reserved for whites. Indeed, racially segregated seating could even offend some whites, when all the white section seats were filled but there were vacant seats in the section set aside for blacks.

In short, racially segregated seating in municipal transit vehicles was seen, by those who owned or managed such companies, as something that reduced profits. Not surprisingly, municipal transit companies in the South fought against the passage of laws requiring racially segregated seating in buses and trolleys. After losing politically in the legislatures, municipal transit companies then took the issue into the courts, where they lost again. And, after the laws went into effect legally, many Southern municipal transit companies simply did nothing to enforce racially segregated seating. In many places, both black and white passengers continued for years to sit wherever they felt like sitting.[25]

Eventually, however, Southern government authorities cracked down. They began charging municipal transit company employees with violations of the law for not enforcing racially segregated seating, and in some cases the owners of those companies were threatened with prosecution if those transit lines did not enforce the racial segregation laws. Only then did the laws that had been passed, in some cases years earlier, finally get enforced.[26]

Railroads were also affected economically by racial segregation laws. When black and white passengers had to be carried in separate coaches, this imposed the considerable cost of buying additional coaches for their passenger trains, as well as the further additional costs of more fuel to move the now heavier trains.

This was especially costly where there were insufficient passengers to fill one coach. If there were only enough black and white passengers for the total to fill two-thirds of the seats in a coach, racial segregation laws could create a situation where there were now two coaches required, each with only one-third of the seats occupied.

Like municipal transit companies, railroad managements in the South opposed the racial segregation laws, in their own self-interest, even if their racial views might not have been any different from those of the politicians who passed such laws. But the incentives to which the politicians responded were votes— that is, white votes— while the incentives to which railroad owners and managers responded were financial, and money was the same, regardless of the racial source.

The famous Supreme Court case of *Plessy v. Ferguson* in 1896 arose from the cooperation of the railroads with Homer Plessy, who was challenging these racial segregation laws, in order to create a test case.

Although Plessy was part of the black community, he was genetically far more Caucasian than African, and was physically indistinguishable from white men. Had he simply gotten on a train and ridden to his destination, there was little likelihood that he would have been questioned about being seated in a railroad car set aside for whites only. But the attorneys for the railroad and the attorneys for Plessy cooperated in arranging a legal confrontation, so that there would be a case to take into the courts.[27] Unfortunately for both, and for the cause of equal rights in general, the Supreme Court majority ruled against them.

There is no predestined outcome of the conflict between economic and political forces. What is important is to recognize the implications of that conflict when crafting or changing laws and policies.

It is not only in political institutions, but also in some economic institutions, that decision-makers are insulated from having to pay the costs of Discrimination II.

Public utility monopolies, whose prices and profit rates are directly controlled by government regulatory agencies, are among the institutions insulated from paying the economic costs which a competitive market imposes on discriminatory behavior, whether directed against ethnic minorities, women or others.

Although engaging in Discrimination II when hiring employees could mean lower profits for a firm operating in competitive markets, a government-regulated public utility that has a monopoly in its market would not be allowed to earn a higher profit rate than the government agency deemed proper in any case. So a regulated public utility company is not forfeiting any additional profit that it would be allowed to keep, if it hired without regard to the group from which job applicants came.

Discrimination II might require the regulated public utility company to pay additional labor costs, because of having to offer higher salaries, in order to attract a larger pool of qualified applicants, from which only applicants from groups that the decision-makers preferred would be hired.* But, for a government-regulated monopoly, such costs can be passed on to customers who have little choice but to pay those costs.

The history of the telephone industry, back when telephones meant land lines, and all the major phone companies in the United States were subsidiaries of the American Telephone and Telegraph Company (A.T.&T.), illustrates this pattern.

As of 1930, there were only 331 black women in the entire country working as telephone operators, out of more than 230,000 women in that occupation. As late as 1950, black women were still only one percent of all women working for phone companies.[28]

However, after creation of "fair employment practices" laws in some Northern states in the 1950s and then federal civil rights laws and policies in the 1960s, many telephone companies reversed their policies, and blacks began to be hired disproportionately.

Prior to the 1960s, however, the state "fair employment practices" laws existed solely outside the South. Although a national sample of employment in the telephone industry showed that the employment of black telephone operators increased more than three-fold between 1950 and 1960,[29] it was 1964 before the first black telephone operator was hired by phone companies in such Southern places as New Orleans, South Carolina or Florida.[30]

Meanwhile, data from a *national* sample of telephone companies showed that blacks accounted for one-third of the total growth in these companies' employees from 1966 to 1968— a trend that had begun in the 1950s and

* A study of employment in government-regulated public utility monopolies, back when that included all telephone companies, pointed out that little worker recruitment was necessary to fill their jobs because, in large cities, "applicants often number in the thousands for a few hundred openings." Bernard E. Anderson, *Negro Employment in Public Utilities: A Study of Racial Policies in the Electric Power, Gas, and Telephone Industries* (Philadelphia: Industrial Research Unit, Wharton School of Finance and Commerce, University of Pennsylvania, 1970), p. 157. Generous pay and benefits also allowed such companies to cherry-pick the enlarged applicant pool for whatever kinds of personalities or other characteristics would make for a more congenial and manageable workforce.

was concentrated mainly in Northeastern and Midwestern companies.[31] But, in the South during the 1950s, in all 11 states that had once formed the Confederate States of America, the share of blacks among male employees of telecommunications companies actually *declined*.[32]

Since all these phone companies were owned and controlled by A.T.& T., such sharp regional disparities in individual phone company policies were far more consistent with regional differences between Southern and non-Southern state governments that regulated these companies than with policies handed down from A.T.&T.'s national management.

What was consistent in all these various regions was that additional costs entailed by either preferential or discriminatory treatment of black job applicants were costs that phone companies could pass on to customers who had little choice but to pay them, since there were only land lines at the time, and each phone company was a monopoly in its own area.

It was much the same story in the government-regulated oil and gas public utilities at that time, where that regulation was also by state agencies, and increased hiring of blacks was confined to states outside the South during that era.[33] These companies too paid no cost for discriminating against blacks before, nor any cost for preferential hiring of blacks afterwards. The same was true of decision-makers who ran non-profit organizations or officials in charge of government hiring policies.

Similar incentives produced similar outcomes in non-profit organizations such as academic institutions, hospitals and foundations— and different outcomes in profit-based businesses operating in competitive markets. Like decision-makers in regulated public utilities, those in non-profit organizations were able to go along with whatever the prevailing opinions and pressures of the time might be, without having to worry about the costs created by Discrimination II against minorities, which their institutions would have to pay.

Against this background, it is hardly surprising that employment discrimination against blacks and Jews was especially widespread among colleges, universities, hospitals and foundations until after World War II, when a revulsion against Nazi racism set in. Before that happened, however, there were 300 black research chemists employed in private businesses in the earlier era, but only three black Ph.D.s in any field employed by white universities.[34]

As for Jews, they were seldom found on American college and university faculties before World War II. Although Milton Friedman had a temporary academic appointment before the war, it lasted only one year, despite high praise for his work by students and colleagues alike, and he spent the war years working as a statistician before eventually becoming a regular, tenured professor of economics at the University of Chicago after the war.[35]

At about the same time, the University of Chicago had its first black tenured professor.[36] The University of Chicago was exceptional only in doing such things *before* most of the rest of the academic world.*

Decades later, after the political climate had changed considerably, colleges and universities engaged in preferential hiring of black faculty, as well as preferential admissions of black students— again, without the academic decision-makers paying any price for their decisions, just as they paid no price for opposite policies earlier. "Affirmative action" in academia was sooner and more sweepingly adopted than in private industries operating in competitive markets.

All this happened too fast for such sweeping policy reversals in non-profit organizations to have been due to changing personnel in the role of decision-makers. In many, if not most, cases the same decision-makers who had discriminated against blacks were now instituting preferential policies favoring blacks. In neither case was the policy necessarily due to the personal beliefs, biases or values of the individual decision-makers, nor was the change necessarily due to "road to Damascus" conversions of personal views occurring among innumerable decision-makers at the same time.

UNINTENDED CONSEQUENCES

In addition to laws and policies directly concerned with Discrimination II, other laws and policies with very different purposes can also change the

---

* As a personal note, the first time I encountered a white professor at a white university with a black secretary, it was Milton Friedman at the University of Chicago in 1960– four years before the Civil Rights Act of 1964.

amount and impact of adverse consequences on groups defined by race, sex or other characteristics. In short, unintended consequences can affect outcomes as readily as intended consequences, and sometimes even more so. Minimum wage laws and building restrictions are two examples among others.

Minimum Wage Laws

Although minimum wage laws in the United States apply without regard to race, that does not mean that their impact is the same on blacks and whites alike. Where rates of pay are determined, not by supply and demand in a free market, but are imposed by minimum wage laws, that can affect the cost of Discrimination II to the discriminator.

A wage rate set above where it would be set by supply and demand in a freely competitive market tends to have at least two consequences: (1) an increase in the number of job applicants, due to the higher wage rate, and (2) a decrease in the number of workers actually hired, due to labor's having been made more expensive. In this situation, the resulting chronic surplus of job applicants beyond the number of jobs available reduces the cost of refusing to hire qualified job applicants from particular groups, so long as the number of qualified job applicants refused employment is not greater than the number of surplus qualified applicants.

When, for example, the number of qualified black job applicants refused employment can be easily replaced by otherwise surplus qualified white or other job applicants, that reduces the cost of Discrimination II to the discriminating employer to virtually zero. On the most basic economic principles, such a situation makes racial or other discrimination far more affordable by employers, and therefore more sustainable, than in a situation where wage rates are determined by supply and demand in a free, competitive market.

In the latter case, where supply and demand leave no chronic surplus or chronic shortage of labor, qualified black job applicants turned away have to be replaced by attracting *additional* other qualified job applicants from other groups by offering higher pay than what that pay would be by supply and demand in a freely competitive and non-discriminatory labor market. In other words, Discrimination II has costs in a free market, greater than its costs when a minimum wage law creates a chronic surplus of job applicants.

Empirical evidence is consistent with this hypothesis. The prevailing national minimum wage law in the United States is the Fair Labor Standards Act of 1938. However, high rates of inflation that began in the 1940s put virtually all money wages above the level specified in that Act, so that for all practical purposes, there was no minimum wage in effect a decade after the law was passed. As economist George J. Stigler pointed out in 1946, "The minimum wage provisions of the Fair Labor Standards act of 1938 have been repealed by inflation."[37]

As of 1948, during this period of no effective minimum wage law, the unemployment rates of both black and white teenagers were just a fraction of what they would become in later years, as minimum wage rates began rising in the 1950s to catch up, and then keep up, with inflation in later years.

What is particularly striking, however, is that there was no significant difference between the unemployment rates of black and white teenagers in 1948. The unemployment rate for black 16-year-old and 17-year-old males was 9.4 percent. For their white counterparts, the unemployment rate was 10.2 percent. For 18-year-old males and 19-year-old males, the unemployment rate was 9.4 percent for whites and 10.5 percent for blacks. In short, there was no significant racial difference in unemployment rates for teenage males in 1948,[38] when there was no effective minimum wage.

After the effectiveness of the minimum wage law was restored by recurring minimum wage increases in later years, not only did teenage unemployment rates as a whole rise to multiples of what they had been in 1948, black teenage male unemployment rates became much higher than the unemployment rates for white teenage males— usually at least twice as high for most years from 1967 on into the twenty-first century.[39]

Labor force participation rates tell much the same story. As of 1955, labor force participation rates were virtually the same for black and white males, aged 16 and 17. For 18-year-old and 19-year-old males, blacks had a slightly higher labor force participation rate than whites, as was also true of males aged 20 to 24. But this pattern changed drastically, as minimum wage rates rose over the years.

In the mid-1950s, black labor force participation rates for 16-year-old and 17-year-old males began falling below that of their white counterparts, and the gap grew wider in succeeding decades. For males aged 18 and 19, the same racial reversal in labor force participation rates occurred a decade later, in the mid-1960s. For males aged 20 to 24, that same racial reversal occurred at the beginning of the next decade, in 1970.

The *magnitude* of the racial difference in labor force participation rates among males, after the racial reversal, followed the same pattern, being greatest for the 16-year-olds and 17-year-olds, less for males aged 18 and 19, and least for males aged 20 to 24.[40]

These labor force participation patterns shed additional light on the basis for racial differences in employment. If the primary reason for that racial difference in labor force participation rates was racism, there was no reason for such reversals, and especially reversals in different years and with different magnitudes for different age groups.

People who are black at age 16 remain black as they get older, so there is no basis for racists to change their treatment of blacks in such patterns as black workers age. But, if the real reason for these patterns was that the work experience and job skills of younger black workers made them less in demand than older black workers with more work experience and/or more job skills, then a rising minimum wage rate prices the younger blacks out of jobs first and to the greatest extent.

Unfortunately, when minimum wage laws reduce the employment prospects of inexperienced and unskilled black teenagers, that reduces their labor force participation, and therefore reduces their rate of acquisition of work experience and job skills. Whatever the degree of racism, it cannot explain age differences in employment among young black males, who do not change race as they grow older.

This pattern of virtually no difference in unemployment rates between black and white teenagers when wages were determined by supply and demand in a free market, but with large and enduring racial differences in unemployment rates when minimum wage laws became effective again, also fits the economic principle that a chronic surplus of job applicants reduces the cost of discrimination to the employer.

This pattern establishes correlation between increased minimum wage rates and changing racial differences in unemployment among teenagers. If this does not conclusively prove causation, it does at least establish a remarkably persistent coincidence.

Alternative explanations for these changing patterns of racial differences— such as racism, poverty or inferior education among blacks— cannot establish even correlation with changing employment outcomes over the years, because all those things were *worse* in the first half of the twentieth century, when the unemployment rate among black teenagers in 1948 was far lower and not significantly different from the unemployment rate among white teenagers.

Building Restrictions

Severe restrictions on building homes or other structures swept through various parts of the United States during the 1970s, in the name of preserving "open space," "saving farmland," "protecting the environment," "historical preservation," and other politically attractive slogans. But, however they were characterized, what such laws and policies did in practice was forbid, or drastically reduce, the building of either housing or other structures. Coastal California, including the entire peninsula from San Francisco to San Jose, was one of the largest regions where severe building-restriction laws and policies arose and prevailed.

The predictable effect of restricting the building of housing, as the population was growing, was a rise in housing prices, when the supply of housing was not allowed to rise as the demand rose. California home prices were very similar to those in the rest of the country before this wave of building restrictions swept across the coastal regions of the state in the 1970s. But, afterward, San Francisco Bay Area home prices rose to more than three times the national average.[41]

In Palo Alto, adjacent to Stanford University, home prices nearly quadrupled during the 1970s, not because more expensive homes were being built— for there were *no* new homes built in Palo Alto during that decade. Existing homes simply skyrocketed in price.[42] By the early twenty-first century, the top ten areas in the United States with the biggest home price increases over the previous five years were all in California.[43]

The racial impact of these housing restrictions was more pronounced than many racially explicit restrictions. By 2005, the black population of San Francisco was reduced to less than half of what it had been in 1970, even though the total population of the city as a whole was growing.[44] In an even shorter span of time, between the 1990 and 2000 censuses, three other California counties— Los Angeles County, San Mateo County, and Alameda County— had their black populations decline by more than ten thousand people each, despite increases in the general population in each of those counties.[45]

By contrast, Harlem was a predominantly white community as late as 1910, and there were openly proclaimed and organized efforts by white landlords and realtors to prevent blacks from moving into Harlem.[46] But, like the organized white efforts to suppress black earnings in the post-bellum South, the mere presence of such organized efforts was no evidence or proof that they achieved their goal. To call such explicitly racist efforts in Harlem unsuccessful would be an understatement.

Those white landlords and realtors in Harlem who held out while others began to rent to blacks, found themselves losing white tenants who moved out of the neighborhood as blacks moved in, leaving the holdouts' buildings with many vacancies, representing lost rent.[47] The collapse of these organized efforts to keep out blacks is hardly surprising under these conditions.

No such economic consequences inhibited those residents and their elected officials in later years who restricted the building of housing in San Francisco and other coastal California communities through the political process, driving up home prices and rents to levels that many blacks could not afford. On the contrary, such restrictions on new building *increased* the market value of the existing homes of residents in those communities and permitted higher rents to be charged by landlords in a market with severe housing shortages.

Attitudes and beliefs, however strongly held or loudly proclaimed, do not automatically translate into end results— into "what emerges"— especially when there are costs to be borne by discriminators themselves.

It may well be that the racial attitudes and beliefs held by white landlords and realtors in early twentieth-century Harlem were more hostile to blacks than the attitudes and beliefs of white residents and officials in late twentieth-century San Francisco and other coastal California areas. But, in terms of end results, the actions of the former failed to keep blacks out of Harlem, while the actions of the latter drove out of San Francisco half the blacks already living in that city. Costs matter.

Chapter 3

SORTING and

UNSORTING PEOPLE

M uch empirical evidence suggests that human beings do not interact randomly— nor as frequently or as intensely— with all other human beings as with selected sub-sets of people like themselves. In short, people sort themselves out, both in where they choose to live and with whom they choose to interact most often and most closely. It is worth examining some of that empirical evidence as to self-sorting, before going on to consider the consequences of third-party sorting or unsorting of other people. The crucial point here is that, when people spontaneously sort themselves, the results are seldom even or random, and are often quite skewed.

RESIDENTIAL SORTING AND UNSORTING

Where people live has, at various times and places, been decided either by the people themselves or by others who imposed various restrictions through a variety of institutional devices, ranging from government laws and policies to many private formal and informal means, ranging from restrictive covenants to homeowners' associations to outright violence against individuals or groups who have sought to live in neighborhoods where they were not welcome.

Residential and Social Self-Sorting

Immigrants have seldom immigrated evenly or randomly from their country of origin. Nor have they settled evenly or randomly in the country they reached. For example, two provinces in mid-nineteenth-century Spain, containing 6 percent of the Spanish population, supplied 67 percent of the Spanish immigrants to Argentina. Moreover, these immigrants tended to live clustered together in particular neighborhoods in Buenos Aires.[1]

Similarly skewed patterns of settlement have been common around the world, among other immigrants moving from their country of origin to their country of settlement. During the era of mass emigration from Italy, for example, Italian immigrants in Australia, Brazil, Canada, Argentina and the United States not only tended to cluster together in predominantly Italian neighborhoods but, more specifically, within those neighborhoods people from Genoa, Naples or Sicily clustered together with other people from those same respective places in Italy.[2]

During that same era, the massive immigration of Eastern European Jews to America was concentrated in New York's Lower East Side. But within those Jewish neighborhoods, Hungarian Jews were largely clustered in their own enclaves, as were Jews from Romania, Russia and other places in Eastern Europe.

German Jews, who had lived in their own enclave on the Lower East Side decades before the mass arrival of Eastern European Jews, were already leaving that neighborhood as they rose socioeconomically, and were increasingly locating in other parts of New York as the Eastern European Jews arrived. Such spatial and social separation between German Jews and Eastern European Jews was common, both in New York[3] and in Chicago.[4]

Lebanese immigrants to Sierra Leone in Africa or Columbia in South America likewise settled in enclaves of other Lebanese from the same parts of Lebanon and of the same religion, with Catholic Lebanese from particular places in Lebanon settling together and separate from enclaves of Orthodox Christians from Lebanon or Lebanese Shiite Muslims.[5]

German immigrants who settled in nineteenth-century New York not only settled in an area of Manhattan called *Kleindeutschland* (little

Germany), Hessians clustered in one part of *Kleindeutschland,* while Prussians clustered in another.[6]

People tend to sort themselves out, not only in their residential patterns but also in their social interactions. Twentieth-century Japanese immigrants to Brazil not only settled in Japanese enclaves, most Okinawan immigrants in Brazil married other Okinawans, rather than marrying Japanese from other parts of Japan, much less marrying members of the Brazilian population at large.[7]

It was much the same story among German immigrants in nineteenth-century New York, where most Bavarians married other Bavarians, and most Prussians married other Prussians. Among the Irish immigrants as well, most nineteenth-century marriages that took place in New York's Irish enclaves were marriages between people from the same county in Ireland.[8]

In the Australian city of Griffith, in the years from 1920 to 1933, 90 percent of Italian men who had emigrated from Venice and gotten married in Australia married Italian women who had also emigrated from Venice. Another five percent married Italian women from other parts of Italy, the same percentage as married "British-Australian" women.[9]

However striking these patterns may be statistically, they are not patterns that most people are made aware of by seeing them with the naked eye, as is the case with differences between black neighborhoods and white neighborhoods in the United States. As a result, black-white residential separations have been seen and treated as if they were unique, as well as being inconsistent with prevailing background assumptions of equal or random outcomes in the absence of discriminatory impositions.

History shows that there have in fact been discriminatory impositions of residential patterns, at various times and places, not only as regards blacks in the United States, but also many other groups in countries around the world. These include the original ghettos imposed on Jews in much of Europe in centuries past. But that does not, by itself, mean that *all* residential sorting and social sorting are externally imposed, or need to be externally eradicated.

Sorting has been as common *within* black neighborhoods as within other neighborhoods around the world. Back in the 1930s, the research of noted black scholar E. Franklin Frazier showed clear patterns of residential clustering of people with different ways of life within the black community in Chicago.

After dividing that community into seven zones, Professor Frazier showed empirically that the proportion of adults to children varied greatly from one zone to another, as did the ratio of males to females, and the percentage of mulattoes in the population was several times higher in one zone than in another.[10]

Moreover, these were not simply isolated differences. They were differences reflecting different socioeconomic levels and differences in family stability and behavioral standards. Delinquency rates within Chicago's black community ranged from more than 40 percent in some neighborhoods to under 2 percent in others.[11]

In nineteenth-century Detroit, black homeowners lived clustered together and separate from black renters.[12] Similar residential differentiation took place in Cleveland's black community.[13] A history of Harlem pointed out occupational differences among people who returned home from work and got off at different subway stops in Harlem.[14]

Mid-twentieth-century data showed income distribution among blacks in the country as a whole to be slightly more unequal than among whites.[15] So did later data.[16] A 1966 study indicated that among the more than 4 million black American families at that time, just 5.2 *thousand* families produced all the black physicians, dentists, lawyers and academic doctorates in the country.[17] Despite how exceptional such occupations and achievements were among blacks at that time, these particular families averaged 2.25 individuals each in those categories.[18] That is, every four such families averaged nine individuals at these levels.

Awareness of such social differences was both widespread and often acute within the black population.[19] There is a whole literature on exclusive black elites, including such books as *Aristocrats of Color* by Willard B. Gatewood, *Our Kind of People* by Lawrence Otis Graham and *Certain People* by Stephen Birmingham.

Particular upscale neighborhoods within mid-twentieth-century Harlem were known as "Strivers' Row" and "Sugar Hill." A luxury apartment building at 409 Edgecombe Avenue was so widely known as a residence of the black elite that it was said to be sufficient to get into a taxi in Harlem and say simply "409" for the driver to know where to take you.[20]

Similar patterns existed in Chicago. There had long been a small black community in Chicago in the nineteenth century, before the great migrations of blacks from the South in the twentieth century led to severalfold increases in the number of blacks in that city. Those blacks born and bred in nineteenth-century Chicago, and living as small enclaves of blacks in an overwhelmingly white population, had over time assimilated culturally to the norms of the surrounding society, as other groups have in similar circumstances.

The later massive migrations of Southern blacks to Chicago in the twentieth century created acute polarization within the black community there.[21] The *Chicago Defender*, a black newspaper, was highly critical of the newcomers for behavior that gave blacks in general a bad name. So were other blacks from the pre-existing black community there and in other Northern cities, where both the existing black residents and the local black press denounced the new arrivals from the South as vulgar, rowdy, unwashed and criminal.[22]

Like other black newspapers in other Northern communities, the *Chicago Defender* published many admonitions to Southern blacks arriving in Chicago, including "Don't use vile language in public places," "Don't allow yourself to be drawn into street brawls," "Don't take the part of law breakers, be they men, women, or children," and "Don't abuse or violate the confidence of those who give you employment."[23]

As with other racial or ethnic groups, in other times and places, blacks in these Northern communities feared that the arrival of less assimilated members of their own race would provoke negative reactions in the larger society that would not only jeopardize the progress of their race, but would even threaten retrogressions, as the larger society turned against blacks in general.[24]

These fears as to how the new black arrivals from the South would behave, and how the local white population would react against blacks in general, both turned out to be all too well founded. A study in early twentieth-century Pennsylvania, for example, showed that the rate of violent crimes among black migrants from the South was nearly five times the rate of such crimes by blacks born in Pennsylvania.[25] The South had long been the country's most violent region, among blacks and whites alike.[26]

Negative reactions from Northern whites set in, as feared, and affected blacks in many ways. Some Northern communities where black children had for years been going to the same schools as white children, now began to impose racial segregation in the schools.[27] In Washington, blacks were no longer allowed in many white theaters, restaurants or hotels, and their opportunities to work in white-collar occupations shrank.[28] There were similar trends in Cleveland and Chicago,[29] among other places. Oberlin College and Harvard, where black students had lived in dormitories with white students before, now excluded black students from their dormitories.[30]

As these retrogressions set in, in Northern cities, black civic organizations, such as the Urban League, sought to assimilate the newcomers to existing norms of behavior, just as civic and religious organizations among the Irish and the Jews did earlier, in order to get Irish and Jewish immigrants assimilated to American cultural standards.

The conclusion that the widespread retrogressions in racial opportunities open to blacks in Northern cities in the early twentieth century were a result of the massive migration of less acculturated Southern blacks to those communities is reinforced by the history of the mass migration of Southern blacks to the Pacific coast, decades later.

In the 1940s, during World War II, industries producing military equipment and supplies on the Pacific coast attracted vast numbers of blacks and whites from the South. Henry Kaiser's huge shipyard in Richmond, California, alone employed more than 90,000 people,[31] and there were similar war industries in other west coast communities.

As among Northern cities in the nineteenth century, blacks were a very small percentage of the population on the Pacific coast before these mass migrations from the South, and were correspondingly more acculturated to the behavioral norms of the surrounding society than were Southern blacks arriving there. Prior to the 1940s, racial discrimination was not on the same scale on the Pacific coast as in the South, or as in Northeastern cities after the great migrations there from the South. In San Francisco, black children went to schools that were not racially segregated and the small black population lived in neighborhoods with whites, Chinese and other races.[32]

The great migrations of blacks out of the South that reached the Northeastern and Midwestern cities around the time of the First World War reached the Pacific coast, decades later, during the Second World War. During the 1940s, more than four-fifths of the blacks who arrived in the San Francisco Bay Area shipyards came from the South, usually the less educated Deep South.[33]

The new black arrivals were overwhelmingly more numerous than the existing black population. In Richmond, California, for example, there were only 270 black residents in 1940 but the Kaiser industries brought in more than 10,000.[34] The black population of Berkeley in the 1950 census was nearly four times what it had been in the 1940 census, before the United States was at war. Over that same span of time, the black population of Oakland rose to more than five times what it had been before, and that of San Francisco rose to approximately nine times its 1940 level.[35]

As in the Northern cities earlier in the twentieth century, the new black arrivals on the west coast were seen by the existing black population there as vulgar and ill-behaved.[36] And, as in Northern cities decades earlier, the arrival of the newcomers was followed by retrogressions in black-white relations.[37]

The Prevalence of Sorting

In countries around the world, innumerable groups have sorted themselves in many ways, both residentially and socially. This sorting extends right down to the individual level. The correlation between the IQs of husbands and wives is at least as high as the correlation between the IQs of brothers and sisters[38]— even though there is no *biological* reason for the IQs of husbands and wives to be similar, as there is with brothers and sisters. Clearly, people sort themselves out when choosing whom to marry, even though they are highly unlikely to actually know the IQ of the person they marry before the wedding, nor necessarily even afterwards. Yet the net result of their spontaneous and informal sorting produces this statistical correlation nevertheless.

There are many kinds of sorting, including sorting by lifestyle in Bohemian neighborhoods like Greenwich Village, which represents an *unsorting* by such other criteria as race or social class origins. Yet what is far harder to find is the even or random distribution of different kinds of people— in places or endeavors— that is widely treated as a norm, deviations from which are regarded as evidence of discrimination, in the sense of Discrimination II.

From the standpoint of particular individuals, there is no question that large, and sometimes devastating, costs can be imposed because of the actions of other members of the group to which they belong, even when the particular individual has played no part in those actions to which members of other groups object.

Such individuals are clearly victims, but of whom? The hooligans and criminals who have caused other groups to seek to protect their own safety and the security of their homes and families? From a moral perspective, there is no obvious "solution," unless the interests of one set of people automatically trump the interests of another, which hardly seems moral, even if it may be politically expedient or in keeping with whatever the social vogues of the time might be.

An episode involving sociologist William Julius Wilson presents a much milder version of the dilemmas faced earlier during the great migrations:

> I am an internationally known Harvard professor, yet a number of unforgettable experiences remind me that, as a black male in America looking considerably younger than my age, I am also feared. For example, several times over the years I have stepped into the elevator of my condominium dressed in casual clothes and could immediately tell from the body language of the other residents in the elevator that I made them feel uncomfortable. Were they thinking, "What is this black man doing in this expensive condominium? Are we in any danger?" I once sarcastically said to a nervous elderly couple who hesitated to exit the elevator because we were all getting off on the same floor, "Not to worry, I am a Harvard professor and I have lived in this building for nine years."

> When I am dressed casually, I am always a little relieved to step into an empty elevator, but I am not apprehensive if I am wearing a tie.
>
> I get angry each time I have an experience like the encounter in the elevator.[39]

Professor Wilson's sarcasm and anger were directed at people whose reactions reflected a greater concern for their own personal safety than for his sensitivities. His account suggests that they were not racists, for merely by wearing a tie he avoided tensions on both sides, even though wearing a tie did not change his race.

Unlike blacks from an earlier era, who clearly blamed those blacks whose behavior had brought on a retrogression that hurt all blacks, Professor Wilson's account gives no indication of any sense that he was paying the social price for dangers created by black hooligans and criminals.

A very different view of such situations was taken by another black scholar, Professor Walter E. Williams, an economist at George Mason University:

> Information is not costless. . . People therefore seek to economize on information cost. In doing so, they tend to substitute less expensive forms of information for more expensive forms. Physical attributes are "cheap" to observe. If a particular physical attribute is perceived as correlated with a more costly-to-observe one, the observer might use that attribute as an estimator or proxy for the costly-to-observe attribute.[40]

In a sense, Professor Wilson's reactions were similar to those of people who blame store owners for the high prices charged in low-income, high-crime neighborhoods, rather than blame those whose behavior raised the costs that the stores' prices have to cover. There was a time when ordinary blacks, with far less education than Professor Wilson, saw clearly that the misbehavior of a black underclass would cause other blacks to be burdened with a backlash.

Imposed Residential and Social Sorting

In addition to spontaneous self-sorting, there is no question that there has also been residential Discrimination II in the plain sense that governmental regulations have explicitly prescribed where people of a particular race, religion, or other social identity can and cannot live.

These would include the original ghettos to which Jews were consigned in particular European cities in centuries past, or whole geographic regions of the Russian Empire where Jews were permitted or not permitted to settle. The areas where Jews were permitted to live were called "the Pale of Settlement"— a phrase surviving in the English language today in statements about certain things being "beyond the Pale."

Similar residential restrictions were placed on the overseas Chinese minorities in various Southeast Asian communities, as well as other groups in other societies around the world. Similar governmental restrictions on where black Americans could live have been common in various forms, supplemented by private racial restrictions.

The question is not whether such residential restrictions can exist, or have existed, but whether the presence of such restrictions can be automatically inferred from statistics showing non-random clusterings of particular people living in particular places or concentrated in particular kinds or levels of particular occupations. Such issues involve not only causal questions but also moral questions— the latter being the hardest to answer.

Causation

Even seeking a causal explanation is by no means simple. We may characterize the behavior of whites who did not want blacks living in their neighborhoods as "racist." But, if we wish to go beyond characterizations to cause and effect, we have entered the world of facts, with its testing of beliefs against evidence. Once again, we confront the difference between Discrimination I and Discrimination II.

Going back to the earliest days of slavery in colonial America, there is no question that slaves simply lived wherever others told them to live. But even in those early times, there were also "free persons of color." In fact, these "free persons of color" existed in the American colonies before slavery, which existed virtually everywhere else in the world, developed as a legal institution in seventeenth-century America.

Before that, the relatively few Africans in the colonies were treated like the far larger numbers of indentured servants from Europe, who were held in bondage for a given number of years, usually to pay off the cost of their passage across the ocean, and then released as free people. In early colonial America, more than half the white population in colonies south of New England arrived as indentured servants.[41]

The relative handful of blacks at that time were treated the same legally, in that regard[42]— but not socially. As the numbers of Africans brought to the colonies increased greatly, their fate became that of perpetual slavery for them and their descendants.

Thus began a cycle of retrogressions followed by progress, followed by new retrogressions followed by new progress, in the treatment of the black population. The reasons for these oscillations tell us something about Discrimination I and Discrimination II.

Even if racist ideas, assumptions and aversions might fully explain discrimination against blacks, that would still leave unexplained these oscillations— which represented major changes, back and forth, lasting for generations, in both the nineteenth century and the twentieth century.

Major restrictions, both legal and social, against "free persons of color" existed in both the North and the South, during the era of slavery. But, while those restrictions tightened over time in the South during the nineteenth century, they eroded in the North during that same century.

In the South, where plantation slavery was the norm, "free persons of color" were seen as dangers to that whole system, both because their very presence demonstrated to slaves that slavery was not an inevitable fate for black people, and because the fraternization of "free persons of color" with slaves not only spread the idea of freedom, but also provided a source of help for slaves who escaped.

In the North, whose climate was not conducive to plantation slavery, and where blacks were a marginal part of the total population, both legal and social restrictions against blacks were not as severe and— more important— began to erode significantly in the second half of the nineteenth century, after successive generations of Northern-born blacks began to acculturate to the behavioral norms of the much larger white population around them.

One indicator of this acculturation to the norms of the larger society was that the black-white difference in homicide rates in various Northern communities during the first half of the nineteenth century was much smaller than it would become a century later. In a monumental treatise on violence in countries around the world, *The Better Angels of Our Nature*, author Steven Pinker noted:

> In the northeastern cities, in New England, in the Midwest, and in Virginia, blacks and whites killed at similar rates throughout the first half of the 19th century. Then a gap opened up, and it widened even further in the 20th century, when homicides among African Americans skyrocketed, going from three times the white rate in New York in the 1850s to almost thirteen times the white rate a century later.[43]

As the small populations of blacks in Northern cities became more acculturated to the norms of the larger society during the nineteenth century, racial barriers began to erode. In Illinois, for example, legal restrictions on access to public accommodations for blacks were removed from the law.[44] There were not enough black voters at that time to have brought this about by themselves, so this represented changes in white public opinion.

In nineteenth-century Detroit, blacks had been denied the right to vote in 1850, but they were voting in the 1880s, and in the 1890s blacks were being elected to statewide offices in Michigan by a predominantly white electorate. The 1880 census showed that, in Detroit, it was not uncommon for blacks and whites to live next door to each other.[45] The black upper class had regular social interactions with upper-class whites, and their children attended high schools and colleges with the children of their white counterparts.[46]

Writing in 1899, W.E.B. Du Bois noted "a growing liberal spirit toward the Negro in Philadelphia," in which the larger community had begun to "brush away petty hindrances and to soften the harshness of race prejudice"— leading, among other things, to blacks being able to live in white neighborhoods.[47] Both contemporary and later writers commented on similar developments in other Northern communities.[48]

While black children in most Northern communities had long been educated in racially segregated schools during the first half of the nineteenth century, if they were allowed to attend public schools at all, this changed during the second half of that century:

> By 1870, those northern states that had excluded blacks from public schools had reversed course. Moreover, during the quarter century following the end of the Civil War, most northern states enacted legislation that prohibited racial segregation in public education. Most northern courts, when called upon to enforce this newly enacted antisegregation legislation, did so, ordering the admission of black children into white schools.[49]

These were not just coincidental mood swings among whites across the North. *The behavior of blacks themselves had changed.* As Jacob Riis put it in 1890, "There is no more clean and orderly community in New York than the new settlement of colored people that is growing up on the East Side from Yorkville to Harlem."[50] By the late nineteenth century, most blacks in New York state had been born in New York state, and grew up with values and behavior patterns similar to those of the vastly larger white population around them.

However, in this as in other things, a major retrogression set in later, in Northern cities, with the arrival of large masses of black migrants from the South in the early twentieth century, concentrated within a relatively few years and arriving in numbers sufficient to prevent their becoming as acculturated to the norms of the larger society, either as quickly or as much as the small nineteenth-century black populations had in the North. The same retrogressions in race relations seen in other aspects of life likewise occurred in Northern schools:

> . . .with the migration of hundreds of thousands of southern blacks into northern communities during the first half of the twentieth century, northern school segregation dramatically increased. Indeed, by 1940, northern school segregation was more extensive than it had been at any time since Reconstruction.[51]

In most cases, this was *de facto* racial segregation in the North, as distinguished from the explicit racial segregation by law in Southern schools. But similar end results were achieved in the North by gerrymandering school districts and by other means. Among the reasons cited for this resurgence of racial segregation in the Northern schools were both educational and behavioral problems of black children.[52] However, as regards educational problems, surveys in both Chicago and Detroit indicated that these were primarily problems with black children whose families had migrated from the South,[53] where educational standards were lower.

Neither eras of progress in race relations nor eras of retrogression were simply inexplicable mood swings among whites. Both represented responses to demonstrable changes in local black populations. These responses were complicated by the inherent problems of white third parties trying to sort out differences among black children, even though sorting out black children in general from white children in general required nothing more than eyesight.

Moreover, in the early twentieth century, the rise to dominance of genetic determinism as a supposedly "scientific" doctrine strengthened the hand of those white officials who were prepared to write off the potential of black and other minority children, as the Progressives of that era did.

UNSORTING PEOPLE

The residential and other outcomes produced by the sorting of people became, in the second half of the twentieth century, widely condemned as wrong in itself, and as creating other social wrongs against the less fortunate groups. This might be considered a special case of the more general assumption that outcomes would tend to be even, or random, in the absence of malign intervention.

But, whatever it was based on, the view became axiomatic among many Americans in the second half of the twentieth century that unsorting people was a high priority, especially in schools, but also in residential neighborhoods.

Educational Unsorting

Perhaps the most famous, and most consequential, Supreme Court decision of the twentieth century was that in *Brown v. Board of Education* in 1954, declaring that racially segregated schools were unconstitutional. This ended more than half a century of hypocrisy, following the 1896 decision in *Plessy v. Ferguson* that government-imposed racial segregation did not violate the Fourteenth Amendment requirement of "equal protection of the laws" for all, so long as the racially segregated facilities provided for blacks were "separate but equal."

For generations, it was widely known that the separate facilities provided for blacks in the racially segregated South were grossly unequal. As courts belatedly began to demand that either equal state institutions be provided for blacks or else blacks must be admitted to the institutions provided for whites, various efforts were made by Southern states to reduce the inequality and, in some cases, blacks were reluctantly granted access to some white institutions, such as a law school in Texas, though with restrictions that did not apply to white students.[54] But even this represented a slow, uphill advance against determined resistance by Southern officials.

Now, in the *Brown v. Board of Education* case, a unanimous Supreme Court decreed that racially segregated schools were, in Chief Justice Warren's words, *inherently* unequal,[55] so that the slow and circuitous route to equalizing government facilities was to be replaced by simply outlawing the official sorting of school children by race.

It was now no longer a question of unequal physical facilities or unequal financial support, for the very act of racial segregation was said to reduce the educational prospects of black children: "To separate them from others of similar age and qualifications solely because of their race generates a feeling of inferiority as to their status in the community that may affect their hearts and minds in a way unlikely ever to be undone."[56]

In the heady atmosphere of the times, where the *Brown v. Board of Education* decision was widely hailed by blacks and most whites alike, except among white Southerners, as a long overdue end to government-imposed racial segregation and discrimination, the ringing assertions made by Chief Justice Warren were widely accepted. Nevertheless, only about a mile from where those pronouncements were made in the Supreme Court, there was an all-black public high school whose history, going all the way back into the nineteenth century, belied the Chief Justice's key assertions about empirical facts.

As of 1954, when Chief Justice Warren declared that separate schools were inherently unequal, all-black Dunbar High School sent a higher percentage of its graduates on to college than any white public high school in Washington.[57] As far back as 1899, when the same tests were given in Washington's four academic high schools at that time, this same all-black public high school scored higher than two of the three white public high schools.[58]

Although most of its graduates went to local colleges, some were already beginning to go to some of the leading colleges in the country at the end of the nineteenth century— and graduating Phi Beta Kappa. Over the period from 1892 to 1954, 34 of these graduates were admitted to Amherst College. Of these, 74 percent graduated from Amherst, and 28 percent of these black graduates were Phi Beta Kappas.[59] Among other elite colleges from which students from this high school graduated Phi Beta Kappa during that era were Harvard, Yale, Williams, Cornell, and Dartmouth.[60]

Among the graduates of this high school— known by various names over the years since its founding in 1870, including Dunbar High School since 1916— were "the first black who" had a range of career achievements. These included the first black woman to earn a Ph.D. at an American university, the first black federal judge, the first black general, the first black Cabinet member, the first black tenured professor at a major national university, and Dr. Charles Drew, who won international recognition as a pioneer in the use of blood plasma.[61]

Clearly, racially segregated schools were *not* inherently inferior. There is no question that most black schools in the South at that time, and many in the North, had inferior educational outcomes. And no doubt inferior resources supplied to black schools had a role in these outcomes, though not necessarily the sole role or the most important role.

In any event, the crusade to racially integrate public schools, during the decades following the *Brown v. Board of Education* decision, generated much social turmoil, racial polarization and bitter backlashes, *but no general educational improvement* from seating black school children next to white school children.

One of the painful ironies of the racial integration crusade was that Dunbar High School's 85 years of academic achievement came to an abrupt end, in the wake of the *Brown v. Board of Education* decision. To comply with that decision, Washington schools were all made neighborhood schools, so that Dunbar could no longer admit black students from anywhere in the city, as it had before, but only students from the particular ghetto neighborhood where it was located. Dunbar quickly became a typical failing ghetto school, with both academic and behavioral problems.

By 1993, a smaller percentage of Dunbar students went on to college than had done so 60 years earlier[62]— even though 1933 was in the depths of the Great Depression of the 1930s and 1993 was in the midst of the prosperous decade of the 1990s.

Neither racial integration nor general prosperity, nor even a newer, more modern and more costly school building was a substitute for what was lost. Yet, toward the end of the twentieth century, some new and highly successful schools brought educational excellence back to many ghetto communities, not only in Washington but also in New York and other communities across the country. Many of these educational successes were in particular chains of charter schools, such as the Success Academy and KIPP (Knowledge Is Power Program) chains.

Not all charter schools were successful, but those that were successful often produced a level of educational achievement far above those of either most ghetto schools or many of the white schools to which black children were bused in the name of racial integration.

Because these highly successful charter schools were often located in low-income black or Hispanic neighborhoods, the demographic makeup of their students was seldom what racial integrationists were seeking. But, nevertheless, educational tests showed that the academic level of students in some of the more successful charter schools located in black ghettos scored well above the national average.

In 2013, children in the fifth grade in one of the Harlem schools in the Success Academy chain "surpassed all other public schools in the state in math, even their counterparts in the whitest and richest suburbs," according to the *New York Times*. Nor was this an isolated fluke. In 2014, children in the Success Academy chain of charter schools as a whole scored in the top 3 percent in English and in the top 1 percent in math.[63]

Although successful charter schools have often been located in low-income minority neighborhoods— and often in the very same buildings where the regular public school children score far below the national average— the successful charter schools are not destroyed by their location, as Dunbar High School had been, when it became a neighborhood school.

Unlike other public schools, charter schools are neither required nor authorized to enroll all the students in their respective neighborhoods. Students are admitted to many or most charter schools by lottery, while most of the local students end up in the regular public school in their neighborhood.

Although admission to these charter schools is by chance, rather than by ability or performance, there is nevertheless a self-sorting of parents and students, with only those parents who want a better education for their children, and only those children willing to subject themselves to a more demanding regimen of school work, being likely to seek admission.

Here, as with Dunbar High School during its past era of academic achievement, *self-sorting* was crucial. Black students were not simply assigned to go to Dunbar High School. They had to apply, and those with neither the interest nor the inclination to subject themselves to rigorous educational norms had no reason to apply.

The educational track record of such self-sorting has been far more successful than *third-party* sorting, whether the third parties sorted by race or by residential location, or by a belief that racial diversity would lead to higher educational achievements.

The self-sorting found among other groups in countries around the world is denied to American blacks when their children are all lumped together, whether by race in the days of the racially segregated South or by residence in public schools with monopolies in their respective districts.

Internal differences have been at least as common among blacks as among other racial or ethnic groups, making self-sorting a way of reducing counterproductive frictions that impede education. Successful charter schools give a glimpse of what can be accomplished by black children in low-income ghettos when self-sorting frees them from the disruptions and violence of unruly classmates, just a small number of whom can prevent a whole class from getting a decent education.

Residential Unsorting

Along with the unsorting of American school children by decades of mandatory busing to racially "integrate" public schools in racially different neighborhoods, there have been parallel efforts to racially "integrate" the neighborhoods themselves.

Among the various government programs to unsort people who have sorted themselves have been programs to build the kind of housing in middle-class neighborhoods that would be affordable to people with lower incomes. Other strategies have included providing subsidies to enable low-income and minority families to be able to rent existing housing in higher income neighborhoods.

The assumption behind such programs has been that social isolation was behind many social pathologies in the ghettos, so that ending that isolation would lead to improvements in the behavior and performances of minority adults and children.

This was essentially the same assumption behind the Supreme Court's *Brown v. Board of Education* decision, that separate facilities were inherently unequal. Although that decision did not explicitly state that racial mixing was essential for black children to get an equal education, that was the logical corollary of what the decision did say.

The idea of racial "integration" or demographic "diversity" spread from education issues to questions of residential unsorting of different racial, ethnic or income groups. Government promotion or imposition of such policies was said to benefit both the newcomers inserted into middle-class neighborhoods and the existing residents who had sorted themselves away from them.

Whatever the plausibility of these assumptions and theories, the crucial question of the empirical validity of these assumptions depends on hard evidence. Contrary to those who attribute social pathologies in the ghettos to external causes in general, and white racism in particular, some of the strongest opposition to government programs that insert people from ghettos into middle-class neighborhoods came from *black* residents in those middle-class neighborhoods.[64] As the *Chicago Tribune* put it:

> The harshest criticism of dispersing public housing's tenants comes not from whites but from blacks. In Harvey, a struggling, working-class African-American suburb south of the city, nearly one of every 10 housing units is already occupied by renters with subsidies.[65]

Among the behaviors of the newcomers commonly complained of by the original residents of working-class and middle-class neighborhoods around the country are that the newcomers' teen-aged children "are allowed to hang out on corners, play basketball late into the night, and sit in parked cars blasting profane music,"[66] as in Chicago. According to pre-existing residents, "they hear frequent gunfire."[67]

In a San Francisco Bay Area community, the charge is that the children of the newcomers are "burglarizing nearby residences, hosting wild parties during the week and weekends, threatening neighbors, and engaging in various forms of criminal activity. . . robbing and assaulting our kids to and from school."[68] In Louisville, homicides have remained concentrated over the years in areas where housing project people have been concentrated.[69]

Black residents in working-class or middle-class communities have been particularly uninhibited in their denunciations of people from housing projects and people on welfare that the government inserts into their communities, perhaps because black middle-class residents are not afraid of being called "racists."

According to the *Chicago Tribune*, the resistance of working-class and middle-class blacks "in some cases has been fierce." Black homeowners have "protested, loudly" at public meetings that they "didn't want 'those people' moving back into their rejuvenated neighborhood." Often homeowners at public gatherings "would shout at officials that they'd worked hard to get where they were and that they didn't want to live next door to people who would just tear up their homes. They called them 'project people,' 'lowlifers' and 'freeloaders.'"[70]

> "Some blacks feel that 'those people' make it tough on those of us trying to make something of ourselves," says Shirley Newsome, a homeowner in Kenwood-Oakland and a longtime voice of moderation. "That's why white America doesn't want me living next to them, because they look at me and figure I'm from a place like public housing."[71]

Like so many social patterns that are usually discussed in terms of race, this pattern of inserting underclass newcomers into neighborhoods where they are resented by the pre-existing residents also exists when the underclass newcomers are white, and are resented by white pre-existing residents. In the best-selling memoir *Hillbilly Elegy*, the author— a white man from a hillbilly background— reported that his grandmother saw the government's placing underclass people in their midst "as a betrayal, ensuring that 'bad' people would move into the neighborhood," even though they "looked a lot like us," but they were the kind of hillbillies who "gave our people a bad name."[72]

Among other things, she resented "the drugs and the late-night fighting" among the new neighbors that the government had placed in their neighborhood, and said of the woman who lived next door: "She's a lazy whore, but she wouldn't be if she was forced to get a job." More pointedly: "I can't understand why people who've worked all their lives scrape by while these deadbeats buy liquor and cell phone coverage with our tax money."[73]

Advocates of unsorting neighborhoods, whether by race or by class, argue that living in a better neighborhood will produce benefits for both the adults and the children who are moved in, and benefits of diversity for society at large. But these expected benefits to the newcomers from housing projects and high-crime neighborhoods have repeatedly failed to show up in extensive empirical studies by a wide variety of researchers on the federal government's "Moving to Opportunity" program.

A study of that program published in the *Journal of Human Resources* concluded: "We did not find evidence of improvements in reading scores, math scores, behavior or school problems, or school engagement, overall or for any age group."[74] Another study of the same program published in the *American Journal of Sociology* concluded that "there is no evidence that extra time spent in low-poverty integrated neighborhoods improves economic outcomes."[75]

Yet another study of the "Moving to Opportunity" program, published in the economic journal *Econometrica* likewise concluded, "we found no significant evidence of treatment effects on earnings, welfare participation, or amount of government assistance after an average of 5 years since random assignment."[76] The *American Economic Review*, the official journal of the American Economic Association, reached similar conclusions about the same federal program— "no consistent detectable impacts on adult economic self-sufficiency or children's educational achievement outcomes" from the movement of thousands of people into higher income neighborhoods than the ones they came from.[77]

The *Quarterly Journal of Economics*, the oldest American journal in economics, likewise concluded that "the changes in neighborhoods induced by MTO ["Moving to Opportunity" program] have not affected the employment rates, earnings, or welfare usage by a statistically detectable amount for household heads."[78]

In addition to these scholarly journals, a study published by the U.S. Department of Housing and Urban Development (HUD) was based on research on that same program which "followed more than 4,600 very low-income families in five U.S. cities over a 10- to 15-year period to examine the short- and long-term effects of moving to low-poverty neighborhoods." Its conclusion was: "No discernible benefit to economic self-sufficiency, employment outcomes, and risky and criminal behavior for adults and children was observed as a result of moving. Similarly, moving had few positive effects on educational achievement for youth."[79]

Nevertheless, Secretary of Housing and Urban Development Shaun Donovan in 2013 "vowed to help urban blacks relocate to suburban neighborhoods, where they can have access to 'good schools, safe streets, jobs, grocery stores,' among other things." Secretary Donovan claimed that realtors and landlords still discriminate against blacks. "African-Americans," Donovan said, "are being denied their freedom of choice."[80] According to *Investor's Business Daily*:

> Earlier this year, HUD broadened the authority of two anti-discrimination laws— the Fair Housing Act and the Equal Credit Opportunity Act— making illegal any housing or credit policy that results in disproportionately fewer blacks or Latinos receiving housing or home loans than whites, even if those policies are race-neutral and evenly applied across all groups.[81]

Here, yet again, we see the implicit assumption that there would be no disparate outcomes unless there were disparate treatment. Moreover, that assumption seems almost impervious to evidence.

One major difference between people sorting or unsorting themselves, on the one hand, and government officials sorting or unsorting them, on the other hand, is that people who sort or unsort themselves receive both the benefits and the costs of doing so. But government officials receive neither the benefits nor the costs of unsorting other people— and so may persist in the process, in utter disregard of benefits or costs that fall on others. Indeed, the *political* costs of admitting to having inflicted socially counterproductive policies are a powerful incentive to keep on inflicting those policies and ignoring or denying their consequences.

It would be wrong to say that there have been literally no benefits at all to anyone from government-subsidized or government-enforced unsorting of people. While some studies have found some benefits to some segments of the low-income groups placed into middle-class neighborhoods by the government,[82] these have seldom, if ever, been of the scope or magnitude envisioned when these programs were instituted.

More fundamentally, negative consequences to the pre-existing residents of the communities into which they have been placed are seldom, if ever, mentioned— much less measured— in these studies. It is as if any benefit, however small, to the new residents automatically outweighs any costs, however large, to the pre-existing residents.

"Disparate Impact" in Employment

Although disparate treatment of individuals, because of the group to which they belong, is what is meant by Discrimination II, this is not always easy to prove in a court of law. Nor does anti-discrimination law, as applied in American courts, require such proof. If a given prerequisite for employment or promotion— a high school diploma, for example— has a "disparate impact" on some group, such as ethnic minorities, then the burden of proof falls on the accused employer to provide a justification of the requirement or else be judged guilty of discrimination.

This process represents a major departure from American legal principles in both criminal and civil cases, where the burden of proof is usually on those making an accusation, rather than expecting the accused to prove their innocence. There are serious practical consequences of this very different legal standard in civil rights cases. There are costs to both employers and workers seeking employment, when the assortment and proportions of employees differ from the assortment and proportions of groups in the surrounding area.

For the employer, the fact that a charge of discrimination can be made solely on the basis of statistics about his employees, without even a single flesh-and-blood human being actually claiming to be discriminated against, means that employers can be put through a costly and time-consuming legal process that can drag on for years, consuming millions of dollars in legal costs alone, quite aside from costs imposed if this uncertain process leads to an unfavorable verdict.

For example, a case charging the Sears department store chain with sex discrimination cost the company $20 million in legal fees[83] and took 15 years to resolve through the federal courts— without the government having to produce even one woman, from any of Sears' hundreds of department stores around the country, claiming to have been discriminated against. Statistical disparities alone were sufficient to keep this costly process going for more than a decade.

In the end, Sears prevailed in the appellate courts. But few employers are in any position to sustain such financial costs for so many years, all the while operating under the public stigma of discrimination accusations that can affect public opinion and the sale of the company's products.

Most employers, including large corporations, find it expedient to settle such cases out of court, even when they have not violated anti-discrimination laws— and the number of such settlements is then used by critics to claim that employment discrimination is widespread. In 2012, for example, PepsiCo paid more than $3 million to settle a charge by the Equal Employment Opportunity Commission that the big soda and snacks company's use of criminal background checks was discrimination against blacks.[84]

This was a bargain compared to the cost to Sears of fighting a charge of discrimination against women, even though Sears eventually won the case. Moreover, having a charge of racial discrimination hanging over PepsiCo for years, while the case dragged on through the federal courts, could have cost more millions, as individuals and institutions decided to buy their sodas and snacks from some other company.

In short, the outcome of "disparate impact" cases does not necessarily depend on either the quantity or the quality of the evidence. By the time of the PepsiCo settlement, an empirical study had already shown that companies using criminal background checks tended to hire *more* blacks than companies which did not use such checks.[85] The crucial factor in such cases is not the trial, but the costliness of going to trial, both in legal fees and in the loss of business due to bad publicity. The only way for the accused to win, in any economically meaningful sense, is for the case to be thrown out of court instead of going to trial.

Rarely does a judge refuse even to let a case go to trial, though that did happen in 2013 when the evidence presented by the Equal Employment Opportunity Commission was called by District Court judge Roger Titus "laughable" because of its "mind-boggling-number of errors" and because of the inconsistency of EEOC's lawsuit against a company for using criminal background checks on job applicants, when the EEOC itself uses such checks.[86]

The implications of the use of a "disparate impact" basis for costly lawsuits in civil rights cases does not end with employers. Workers can also be adversely affected, and not just with reduced employment opportunities for black workers who have no criminal record.

When a federal agency can so easily make charges of discrimination on behalf of workers from racial or ethnic minorities— charges that can be costly and time-consuming to defend against in the courts, or charges that can force costly settlements out of court— that reduces the value of hiring black or other minority workers, even when their job qualifications are equal to the job qualifications of other workers who present no such legal risk.

Employers therefore have incentives to locate their businesses away from concentrations of minority populations, so that they will not be as legally vulnerable to costly charges of discrimination if their work force does not end up with the same demographic makeup as that of the surrounding population.

Japanese firms seeking to find locations for their first businesses in the United States have specified that they do not want to locate near concentrations of blacks in the local population.[87] American firms that do the same thing, being more familiar with both the legal and the social atmosphere in the United States, may be less likely to leave a paper trail. Nevertheless, this raises the question whether anti-discrimination laws, as applied in the courts, provide incentives to discriminate against racial minorities as well as incentives not to discriminate, with their net effect being uncertain.

Many observers who see racism as both widespread and widely effective in the job market fail to account for the fact that employers in competitive markets have actively sought out black workers, even in places and times where racism was rampant and undisguised, such as in South Africa during the era of apartheid, under a white minority government openly proclaiming white supremacy.

Similarly, black American workers were sufficiently in demand more than a century ago, in the Jim Crow South, that the organized attempts of white employers and landowners to suppress black earnings often collapsed under the pressure of that demand for black workers and sharecroppers.

Northern white employers sent recruiters into the South during the Jim Crow era to recruit black workers, on such a scale as to cause many laws to be passed in the South, restricting the activities of these recruiters by charging them licensing fees and imposing other restrictions, and with serious penalties for violating those restrictions.[88] This clearly indicated a strong demand for black workers in both regions of the country.

Within Northern communities, the demand for black workers was sufficient in the 1920s to cause Henry Ford and his executives to establish connections with clergy in Detroit's black community, in order to get their help in sorting black job applicants. Similar arrangements existed in Chicago and Pittsburgh.[89] The Ford Motor Company was, in effect, seeking low-cost access to knowledge of individual qualities, in order to judge each individual individually, instead of having to rely on information about group characteristics.

In short, racism has not been sufficient to prevent a demand for black workers in a competitive market. It would be painfully ironic if anti-discrimination laws have been among the factors which reduced that demand in later times. Intentions, whether good or bad, do not predestine outcomes.

Chapter 4

THE WORLD OF

NUMBERS

When trying to understand economic and social disparities, statistics are often used, both to convey the magnitude of those disparities and to try to establish their causes. To some, numbers may convey a sense of objective, hard facts. But, even when the numbers are correct, the words that describe what the numbers are measuring may be incorrect or misleading. These include such basic numbers as income, unemployment rates and rates of arrest for violations of laws.

Numbers may also be misleading, not because of any intrinsic defects in either the numbers themselves or in the words describing them, but because of implicit assumptions about the norms to which those numbers are being compared. Here the seemingly invincible fallacy of assuming an even or random distribution of outcomes as something to expect, in the absence of such complicating causes as genes or discrimination, can make many statistics that show very disparate outcomes be seen as indicating something fundamentally wrong in the real world, rather than something fundamentally wrong with the assumptions behind the norms to which those outcomes are being compared.

Neither logic nor empirical evidence provides a compelling reason for expecting either equal or random outcomes among individuals, groups, institutions or nations.

When used with an awareness of their pitfalls, statistics can be enormously valuable in testing competing hypotheses about disparate outcomes. But statistics may nevertheless be grossly misleading when they are distorted by errors of omission or errors of commission.

ERRORS OF OMISSION

The mere omission of one crucial fact can turn accurate statistics into traps that lead to conclusions that would be demonstrably false if the full facts were known. This often happens in comparisons of different ethnic groups and different income classes, among other comparisons.

Group Disparities

During a long and heated campaign in politics and in the media during the early twenty-first century, claiming that there was rampant discrimination against black home mortgage loan applicants, data from various sources were cited repeatedly, showing that black applicants for the most desirable kinds of mortgages were turned down substantially more often than white applicants for those same mortgages.

In the year 2000, for example, data from the U.S. Commission on Civil Rights showed that 44.6 percent of black applicants were turned down for those mortgages, while only 22.3 percent of white applicants were turned down.[1] These and similar statistics from other sources set off widespread denunciations of mortgage lenders, and demands that the government "do something" to stop rampant racial discrimination in mortgage lending institutions.

The very same report by the U.S. Commission on Civil Rights, which showed that blacks were turned down for conventional mortgages at twice the rate for whites, contained other statistics showing that whites were turned down for those same mortgages at a rate nearly twice that for "Asian Americans and Native Hawaiians."

While the rejection rate for white applicants was 22.3 percent, the rejection rate for Asian Americans and Native Hawaiians was 12.4 percent.[2] But such data seldom, if ever, saw the light of day in most newspapers or on most television news programs, for which the black-white difference was enough to convince those journalists that racial discrimination was the reason.

This conclusion fit existing preconceptions, apparently eliminating a need to check whether it also fit the facts. This one crucial omission enabled the prevailing preconception to dominate discussions in politics, in the media and in much of academia.

One of the very few media outlets to even consider alternative explanations for the statistical differences was the *Atlanta Journal-Constitution*, which showed that 52 percent of blacks had credit scores so low that they would qualify only for the less desirable subprime mortgages, as did 16 percent of whites. Accordingly, 49 percent of blacks in the data cited by the *Atlanta Journal-Constitution* ended up with subprime mortgages, as did 13 percent of whites and 10 percent of Asians.[3]

But such statistics, so damaging to the prevailing preconception that intergroup differences in outcomes showed racial discrimination, in the sense of Discrimination II, were almost never mentioned in most of the mass media.

The omitted statistics would have undermined the prevailing preconception that white lenders were discriminating against black applicants. However, that preconception at least seemed plausible, even if it failed to stand up under closer scrutiny. But the idea that white lenders would also be discriminating against white applicants, and in favor of Asian applicants, lacked even plausibility. What was equally implausible was that black-owned banks were discriminating against black applicants. But in fact black-owned banks turned down black applicants for home mortgage loans at a *higher* rate than did white-owned banks.[4]

Household Income Statistics

It is, unfortunately, not uncommon to omit statistics that are discordant with prevailing preconceptions. This has become a common practice in politics, in the media and even in much of academia. Such errors of omission are not confined to mortgage loan issues, but are also common in many discussions of income statistics.

Household income data, for example, are often used to indicate the magnitude of economic disparities in a society. But to say that the top 20 percent of households have X times as much income as the bottom 20 percent of households exaggerates the disparity between flesh-and-blood human beings, which can be quite different from disparities between income brackets. That is because, despite equal numbers of *households* in each 20 percent, there are far more *people* in the top 20 percent of households.

Census data from 2002 showed that there were 40 million people in the bottom 20 percent of households and 69 million people in the top 20 percent of households.[5] Such facts are usually omitted in statistics about disparities in incomes.

No doubt people in the top quintile average higher incomes than people in the bottom quintile. But the fact that there were also 29 million more people in this top quintile exaggerates the disparity in incomes among *people*. Later data for 2015 from the U.S. Bureau of Labor Statistics indicated that there were now over 36 million more people in the top quintile than in the bottom quintile.[6] Moreover, the number of people earning income was four times as great in the top quintile as in the bottom quintile.[7] That is yet another of the errors of omission, when the truth would undermine a prevailing preconception.

There are not only different numbers of people per household at different income levels, there are also different numbers of people per household from one ethnic group to another, and different numbers of people per household from one time period to another. Omitting those differences when drawing conclusions can distort the meaning or implications of those statistics.

As the Bureau of the Census pointed out, more than half a century ago, the number of households has been increasing faster than the number of people.[8] In short, American households tend to contain fewer people per household over time— a trend continuing into the twenty-first century.[9] There are not only smaller families in later times, more individuals are financially able to live in their own individual households, rather than live with relatives or roommates, or live as individual roomers or in boarding houses, as average incomes rise from generation to generation.

When income per person is rising over the same span of years when the average number of persons per household is declining, that can lead to statistics indicating that the average household income is *falling*, even if all individual incomes are *rising*.

For example, if per capita income rises by 25 percent over some span of years, during which the average number of persons per household declines from 6 persons to 4 persons, then four people in the later period have as much income as five people had in the earlier period. But that is still less income than *six* people had in the earlier period, so average household income *falls*, statistically, even if income per person has risen by 25 percent.

Household income statistics can be misleading in other ways. If two low-income people are sharing an apartment, in order to make the cost of rent less burdensome to each, and if either or both has an increase in salary, that can lead to one tenant moving out to live alone in another apartment— and that, in turn, can lead to a *fall* in average household income.

If, for example, each of the two tenants has an income of $20,000 a year, and later both reach an income of $30,000 a year, leading to each living in a separate apartment afterwards, that will mean a *fall* in household income for these individuals from $40,000 a year to $30,000 a year. There will now be two low-income households instead of one, and each household will be poorer than the one they replaced. Again, a rise in individual income can be reflected statistically as a fall in household income.

Since most income is paid to individuals, rather than to households, and "individual" always means one person while "household" can mean any changeable number of persons, why would household income statistics be used so often instead of individual income statistics?

Clearly, omitting individual income statistics, and using household income statistics instead, is less useful to someone seeking the truth about economic differences among human beings. But household income statistics can be very useful for someone promoting political or ideological crusades, based on statistics that exaggerate income disparities among people.

Time and Turnover

Another factor often omitted, or distorted, in discussions of income disparities is the *time* dimension. People in the bottom 20 percent are often spoken of as "the poor" and, if the income in that quintile has not changed much over some span of years, it may be said that the income of "the poor" has stagnated. But the great majority of people initially in the bottom quintile do not stay there permanently.

Most of the people in that bottom quintile initially are likely to be gone in later years, precisely because their incomes have *not* stagnated— and our concern is for the fate of flesh-and-blood human beings, not the fate of abstract statistical categories.

A University of Michigan study that followed a given set of working Americans from 1975 to 1991 found that 95 percent of the people initially in the bottom 20 percent were no longer there at the end of that period. Moreover, 29 percent of those initially in the bottom quintile rose all the way to the top quintile, while only 5 percent still remained in the bottom 20 percent.[10]

Since 5 percent of 20 percent is one percent, only one percent of the total population sampled constituted "the poor" throughout the years studied. Statements about how the income of "the poor" fared during those years would apply only to that one percent of the people.

Similar distortions of reality occur when the time dimension is ignored in discussing people in the upper income brackets, who are often also spoken of as if they were an enduring class of people, rather than transients in those brackets, just like "the poor" in lower brackets. Thus a *New York Times* essay in 2017 referred to "This favored fifth at the top of the income distribution" as having collected "since 1979" a far greater amount of income than others.[11]

Considering how much turnover there was among people in different quintiles from 1975 to 1991, the implicit assumption that there were the same people in the top quintile over the even longer period from 1979 to 2017 is a staggering assumption. But of course the very idea of turnover was omitted.

Another of the relatively few statistical studies that followed a given set of Americans over a span of years found a reality very different from what is usually portrayed in the media, in politics, or in academia: "At some point between the ages of 25 and 60, over three-quarters of the population will find themselves in the top 20 percent of the income distribution."[12] For most Americans in other quintiles to envy or resent those in the top quintile would mean envying or resenting *themselves*, as they will be in later years.

Calling people in particular income brackets "the poor" or "the rich" implicitly assumes that they are enduring residents in those brackets, when in fact most Americans do not stay in the same income quintile from one decade to the next.[13]

The turnover rate among people in the highest income brackets is even greater than that of the population in general. Fewer than half the people in the much-discussed "top one percent" in income in 1996 were still there in 2005. People initially in the top *one hundredth of one percent* had an even faster turnover, and those with the 400 highest incomes in the country turned over fastest of all.[14]

Crime Statistics and Arrest Statistics

Some of the most gross distortions of reality through errors of omission have involved quite simple omissions. No one needs to be an expert on the complexities of statistics in order to see through many statistical fallacies, including those based on simple omissions. But it does require stopping to think about the numbers, instead of being swept along by a combination of statistics and rhetoric.

Statistics cited in support of claims that the police target blacks for arrests usually go no further than showing that the proportion of black people arrested greatly exceeds the roughly 13 percent of the American population who are black.

If anyone were to use similar reasoning to claim that National Basketball Association (NBA) referees were racially biased, because the proportion of fouls that referees call against black players in the NBA greatly exceeds 13 percent, anyone familiar with the NBA would immediately see the fallacy—

because the proportion of black players in the NBA greatly exceeds the proportion of blacks in the American population.

Moreover, since blacks are especially over-represented among the star players in the NBA, the actual playing time of black players on the floor would be even more disproportionately higher, and it is the players on the floor who get cited for fouls more so than secondary players sitting on the bench.

What would be relevant to testing the hypothesis that blacks are disproportionately targeted for arrest by the police, or disproportionately convicted and sentenced by courts, would be objective data on the proportions of particular violations of the law committed by blacks, compared to the proportions of blacks arrested, convicted and sentenced for those particular violations.

Such objective data are not always easy to come by, since data reflecting actions by the police would hardly be considered valid as a test of whether the actions of the police were warranted. However, there are some particular statistics that are both relevant and independent of the actions of the police.

The most reliable and objective crime statistics are statistics on homicides, since a dead body can hardly be ignored, regardless of the race of the victim. For as long as homicide statistics have been kept in the United States, the proportion of homicide victims who are black has been some multiple of the proportion of blacks in the population. Moreover, the vast majority of those homicide victims whose killers have been found were killed by other blacks, just as most white homicide victims were killed by other whites.

Since the homicide rate among blacks is some multiple of the homicide rate among whites, it is hardly surprising that the arrest rate of blacks for homicide is also some multiple of the rate of homicide arrests among whites. It has nothing to do with the proportion of blacks in the general population, and everything to do with the proportion of blacks among people who commit a particular crime.

Another violation of the law that can be tested and quantified, independently of the police, is driving in excess of highway speed limits. A study by independent researchers of nearly 40,000 drivers on the New Jersey

Turnpike, using high-speed cameras and a radar gun, showed a higher proportion of black drivers than of white drivers who were speeding, especially at the higher speeds.[15]

This study, comparing the proportion of blacks stopped by state troopers for speeding with the proportion of blacks actually speeding, was not nearly as accepted, or even mentioned, either by the media or by politicians, as other studies comparing the number of blacks stopped by state troopers for speeding and other violations with the proportion of blacks in the *population*.[16]

Yet again, specific facts have been defeated by the implicit presumption that groups tend to be similar in what they do, so that large differences in outcomes are treated as surprising, if not sinister. But demographic differences alone are enough to lead to group differences in speeding violations, even aside from other social or cultural differences.

Younger people are more prone to speeding, and groups with a younger median age have a higher proportion of their population in age brackets where speeding is more common. When different groups differ in median age by a decade, or in some cases by two decades or more,[17] there was never any reason to expect different groups to have the same proportion of their respective populations speeding, or to have the same outcomes in any number of other activities that are more common in some age brackets than in others.

The omission of data on the proportion of blacks— or any other racial group— engaged in a given violation of law, as distinguished from the proportion of blacks or others in the population at large, is sufficient to let racial profiling charges prevail politically, despite their inconsistency with either logic or evidence.

Some professional statisticians have refused to get involved in "racial profiling" issues. As a professor of criminology in North Carolina explained: "Good statisticians were throwing up their hands and saying, 'This is one battle you'll never win. I don't want to be called a racist.'"[18]

Among the other consequences is that many law enforcement officials also see this as a politically unwinnable battle, and simply back off from vigorous law enforcement, the results of which could ruin their careers and their lives. The net result of the police backing off is often a rise in crime,[19] of which law-abiding residents in black communities are the principal victims.

Some people may think that they are being kind to blacks by going along with unsubstantiated claims of "racial profiling" by the police. But, as distinguished black scholar Sterling A. Brown said, long ago: "Kindness can kill as well as cruelty, and it can never take the place of genuine respect."[20]

ERRORS OF COMMISSION

Statistical errors of commission include lumping together data on things that are fundamentally different, such as salaries and capital gains, producing numbers that are simply called "income."

Other errors of commission include discussing statistical brackets as if they represented a given set of flesh-and-blood human beings called "the rich," "the poor" or "the top one percent," for example. Errors of commission also include using survey research to resolve factual issues that the inherent limitations of survey research make it unable to resolve.

Capital Gains

While annual income statistics for individuals avoid some of the problems of household income statistics, both of these sets of statistics count as income (1) annual salaries earned in a given year and (2) income from capital gains accrued over some previous span of years, and then turned into cash income during a given year. Treating the incomes earned by some individuals over various numbers of years as being the same as incomes earned by other individuals in just one year is like failing to distinguish apples from oranges.

Capital gains take many forms from many very different kinds of transactions. These transactions range from sales of stocks and bonds that may have been bought years earlier to sales of a home or business that has increased in value over the years.

If a farm was purchased for $100,000 and then, 20 years later— after the farmer has built barns and fences, and made other improvements to the land

and the structures on it— the farm is then sold for $300,000, that sale will result in a net increase of the owner's income by $200,000 in the particular year when the farm is sold. Statistically, that $200,000 that was earned over a period of 20 years will be recorded the same as a $200,000 salary earned by someone else in just one year.

Looking back, that farmer has in reality earned an average of $10,000 a year for 20 years as increases in the value of the farm, through the investment of time, work and money on the farm. Looking forward, the farmer cannot expect to earn another $200,000 the following year, as someone with a $200,000 annual salary can.

Capital gains in general are recorded in income statistics as being the same as an annual salary, when clearly they are not. Nor is there some easy formula available to render salaries and capital gains comparable, because capital gains by different individuals accrue for differing numbers of years before being turned into cash income in a given year.

If capital gains were equally present at all income levels— say, 10 percent of all incomes being capital gains— then the disparities in income statistics might not be affected much. But, in reality, low annual incomes are far more likely to be salaries and very high annual incomes are far more likely to be capital gains. While people making twenty *thousand* dollars a year are probably getting that from a salary, people making twenty *million* dollars a year are more likely to be making such a sum of money from capital gains of one sort or another.

The exceptionally high rates of turnover of people at very high income levels reinforce this conclusion. Internal Revenue Service data show that half the people who earned over a million dollars a year, at some time during the years from 1999 and 2007, did so just *once* in those nine years.[21]

This does not imply that all the others in that bracket made a million dollars every year. Another study, also based on tax data, showed that, among Americans with the 400 highest incomes in the country, fewer than 13 percent were in that very high bracket more than twice during the years from 1992 to 2000.[22] The highest incomes are usually very transient incomes, reinforcing the conclusion that these are transient capital gains rather than enduring salaries.

All of this distorts the implications of income statistics that treat annual salaries and multi-year capital gains as if they were the same. Talk of how much of a country's income is received by the top ten percent, or top one percent, proceeds as if this is a given set of people when, because of the high turnover in high income brackets, there can be thousands of people in the "top 400" during just one decade. When incomes received by thousands of people are reported statistically as if these were incomes received by hundreds of people, that is a severalfold exaggeration of income disparities.

SIDEBAR: CAPITAL GAINS AND INEQUALITY

A hypothetical example may illustrate how income statistics can exaggerate inequality when they make no distinction between (1) people who receive annual salaries in a given year and (2) people who receive capital gains in that same year, representing income earned over a previous span of years.

If, for example, there are 10 people who are in a high income bracket, each earning $500,000 a year, while there are also 10 people in a lower income bracket, each earning $50,000 a year, it might seem as if there is a ten-to-one difference in income between people in these two brackets. But, if only one of the ten people in the higher bracket is earning $500,000 *every* year in a decade, while the others are there for just one year each in that decade— the year in which their accrued capital gains are turned into cash income— then given the very high rate of turnover in very high income brackets, the situation is very different from what it would be if there were the same ten people in the higher bracket every year of the decade.

If most of the people in the higher income bracket have a one-year spike in income from capital gains, after which they return to some lower level of income, which may still be above the national average— say, an individual income of $100,000 a year— then, over the course of a decade, the income disparity between *people* is substantially less than the income disparity between *income brackets*.

In this hypothetical example, where there are nine people initially in the higher income bracket, earning $500,000 each in the first year covered, and $100,000 in each of the subsequent nine years of the decade, that adds up to a total of $1.4 million each during that decade, which in turn adds up to $12.6 million for all nine people collectively. The tenth member of the top bracket, who is in that bracket every year of the decade, receiving $500,000 a year in all ten years, has a total income of $5 million. For all these particular ten people put together, that adds up to $17.6 million received collectively in a decade by the ten people initially in the higher bracket.

Meanwhile, among the ten people in the lower income bracket, receiving $50,000 a year each initially and throughout the decade, that adds up to $500,000 each in a decade, for a total income of $5 million as a group. With the ten people initially in the higher bracket earning a total of $17.6 million during that same decade, and the ten people initially in the lower bracket earning a total of $5 million during that decade, the disparity in income between *people* is less than four-to-one, while the disparity in income between their respective income *brackets* is ten-to-one.

That is because nine of the ten people in the higher bracket are replaced each year by someone else having a one-year spike in income from capital gains, for an income of $500,000 in this example. Counting all 91 people who are in the higher income bracket at some point during the decade, their average annual incomes are less than *three* times that of people in the lower bracket.[23]

Although this exercise assumes, for the sake of simplicity, that people in the lower income bracket have constant incomes throughout the decade, data from the real world show the incomes of people initially in lower income brackets to usually be rising over time more sharply than the incomes of people initially in higher brackets.[24] This would make the disparity in incomes between people in these two brackets even less than that in this example.

A hypothetical example cannot pretend to be an exact replica of the real world. The point is merely to illustrate how, under some approximation of these conditions, the disparities between income brackets can be much greater than the disparities between actual flesh-and-blood human beings.

Racial and Ethnic Disparities

In trying to determine the reasons for economic and social disparities between blacks and whites, some observers attribute these differences primarily to policies and practices by people outside the black community, while other observers attribute these same differences to internal differences in behavior between black and white Americans.

In seeking to resolve this issue, sociologist William Julius Wilson relied heavily on statistics from opinion surveys. These surveys, according to Professor Wilson, show that "nearly all ghetto residents, whether employed or not, support the norms of the work ethic."[25] In one survey, "fewer than 3 percent of the black respondents from ghetto poverty census tracts denied the importance of plain hard work for getting ahead in society, and 66 percent expressed the view that it is very important."[26]

After admitting that "surveys are not the best way to get at underlying attitudes and values,"[27] Professor Wilson nevertheless presents— as a refutation of "media perceptions of 'underclass' values and attitudes" in inner-city ghettos— the fact that "residents in inner-city ghetto neighborhoods actually verbally endorse, rather than undermine, the basic American values concerning individual initiative."[28]

Despite William Julius Wilson's reliance on opinion surveys to refute claims that ghetto residents have different cultural values from those of the American population as a whole, there is no necessary correlation between what people say and what they do. A survey of low-income people by Columbia University researchers showed that 59 percent regarded buying goods on credit as a bad idea. Nevertheless "most of the families do use credit when buying major durables."[29]

The difference between survey results and demonstrable realities was also pointed out by the author of *Hillbilly Elegy*: "In a recent Gallup poll, Southerners and Midwesterners reported the highest rates of church attendance in the country. Yet *actual* church attendance is much lower in the South."[30] He also found another survey, indicating that working-class whites worked more hours than college-educated whites to be "demonstrably false."[31] Those who did the survey "called around and asked people what they thought. The only thing that report proves is that many folks talk about working more than they actually work."[32]

If someone with no pretensions of being an academic scholar could see the tenuous relationship between survey results and the realities of life, it is hard to understand why surveys were relied on by Professor Wilson for deciding such a crucial issue as the internal or external sources of racial differences in socioeconomic outcomes.

Economists tend to rely on "revealed preference" rather than verbal statements. That is, what people *do* reveals what their values are, better than what they *say*. Even when people give honest answers, expressing what they sincerely believe, some people's conception of hard work, for example, need not coincide with other people's conception, even when both use the same words.

When black students in affluent Shaker Heights spent less time on their school work than their white classmates did, and spent more time watching television,[33] that was their revealed preference. Nor are black and white Americans the only groups with different revealed preferences. In Australia, for example, Chinese students have spent more than twice as much time on their homework as white students did.[34]

How surprised should we be that Asian students in general tend to do better academically than white students in general, *in predominantly white societies* such as Australia, Britain or the United States? The same pattern can be seen among whole nations, as such Asian countries as Japan, Korea and Singapore likewise show patterns of hard work by their students and academic results on international tests that place these countries well above most Western nations.[35]

Statistics compiled from what people say may be worse than useless, if they lead to a belief that those numbers convey a reality that can be relied on for serious decision-making about social policies.

Incidentally, the high correlation between the amount of work that different groups put into their education and the quality of their outcomes does not bode well for theories of genetic determinism. When we find some race whose lazy students get educational results superior to the results of hard-working students in other races, this would be evidence supporting that hypothesis, but such evidence does not seem to be available.

Minimum Wages and Unemployment

One of the important areas in which survey research has done major damage has been in trying to resolve differences of opinion as to the effect of minimum wage laws on unemployment. Advocates of minimum wage laws argue that such laws raise the income of the poor, while critics argue that these laws cause more of the poor to be unemployed, because low-income workers tend to be workers with few skills and/or little work experience, so that employers find them worth employing only at low wage rates. Despite an abundance of detailed statistics on unemployment, this controversy has raged for generations.

Part of the problem is that, as we have seen in other contexts, most of what are called "the poor" are not permanent residents in low-income brackets, any more than other people are permanent residents in other income brackets. Most of the people being paid the minimum wage rate are young workers, and of course they do not remain young over the years. So, when people say, as Senator Ted Kennedy once said, "Minimum wage workers have waited almost 10 long years for an increase,"[36] they are not talking about a given set of human beings, but about a statistical category containing an ever-changing mix of people.

Because young people are usually, almost by definition, less experienced as workers, their value to a prospective employer tends to be less than the value of more experienced workers in the same line of work. Some young people may acquire valuable work skills through education, but education also takes time, and people grow older with the passage of that time.

Often what younger, inexperienced workers acquire from an entry-level job is primarily the habit of showing up every day and on time, and the habit of following instructions and getting along with others. But, simple as such things may seem, the absence of these prerequisites can negate whatever other good qualities a young worker may have.

After having acquired work experience in some simple, entry-level job, most young beginners go on to other jobs where work experience of some sort may be a prerequisite for getting hired.

High rates of employee turnover, sometimes exceeding 100 percent per year, are common in many entry-level jobs in retail businesses or fast-food restaurants.[37] These jobs are stepping stones to other jobs with other employers, though some observers falsely call entry-level jobs "dead-end jobs."

If workers in fact stayed on permanently in such jobs, which usually have no automatic promotions ladder, those workers would in fact be in dead-end jobs. But, when the average tenure of supermarket employees has been found to be 97 days, that is clearly not the case.[38]

Like most things in a market economy, inexperienced and unskilled workers are more in demand at a lower price than at a higher price. Minimum wage laws, based on what third parties would like to see them paid, rather than being based on productivity, can price unskilled workers out of a job.

This traditional economic analysis has been challenged by advocates of minimum wage laws, and survey research data has been a major part of that challenge.

Back in 1945, Professor Richard A. Lester of Princeton University sent out questionnaires to employers, asking how they would respond to higher labor costs. Their responses, which were not along the lines of traditional economic analysis, convinced Professor Lester that the traditional economic analysis was either incorrect or not applicable to minimum wage laws.[39]

However, what traditional economic analysis seeks to do is predict economic outcomes, not predict how people will answer questionnaires. Moreover, outcomes are not just the fruition of beliefs or intentions, as we have seen in discussions of the costs of discrimination.

Decades after Professor Lester's challenge to traditional economic analysis, other economists, also at Princeton, again challenged traditional economic analysis on the basis of survey research, though this time by surveying the same employers before and after a minimum wage increase, and asking each time how many employees they had. The answers convinced the Princeton economists that the minimum wage increase had not reduced employment. They and their supporters therefore declared the traditional analysis to be a "myth."[40]

Devastating criticisms of the Princeton economists' conclusions were made by other economists, who challenged both the accuracy of their statistics and the logic of their conclusions.[41] But, even if the Princeton economists' statistics were accurate, that would still not address the key weakness of survey research in general— which is that *you can only survey survivors*. And what may be true of survivors need not be true of others in the same circumstances who did not survive in those particular circumstances.

An extreme hypothetical example may illustrate the point that is applicable in less extreme situations. If you wished to determine whether playing Russian roulette was dangerous, and did so through survey research, you might send out questionnaires to all individuals known to have played Russian roulette, asking them for information as to their outcomes.

After the questionnaires were returned and the answers tabulated, the conclusion from these statistics might well be that no one was harmed at all, judging by the answers on the questionnaires that were returned. Not all questionnaires would have been returned, but that is not uncommon in survey research. Basing your conclusions on the statistical data from this research, you might well conclude that you had disproved the "myth" that playing Russian roulette was dangerous. This is the kind of result you can get when you can only survey survivors.*

In the case of minimum wage studies, if all the firms in an industry were identical, then any reduced employment resulting from the imposition of a minimum wage, or the raising of an existing minimum wage rate, would appear as a reduction of employment in all the firms. But, in the more usual case, where some firms in a given industry are quite profitable, others are less profitable and still others are struggling to survive, unemployment resulting from a minimum wage can push some struggling firms out of the industry— and reduce the number of their replacements, now that labor costs are higher and profits more problematical.

---

* Professor George J. Stigler, in a critique of Professor Lester's survey research, not long after World War II, pointed out that "by parallel logic it can be shown by a current inquiry of health of veterans in 1940 and 1946 that no soldier was fatally wounded." George J. Stigler, "Professor Lester and the Marginalists," *American Economic Review*, Vol. 37, No. 1 (March, 1947), p. 157.

The only firms that can be surveyed for their employment data, both before and after the minimum wage was imposed or raised, are the firms that were there in both time periods— that is, the survivors. If there has been a net decrease in the number of firms, the employment in these surviving firms need not have gone down at all, regardless of a decline in employment in the industry as a whole. The firms surveyed are like the people who survived playing Russian roulette, which may well be a majority in both cases, though not an indicative majority.

Empirically, a study of the effect of minimum wages on employment in restaurants in the San Francisco Bay Area found that the principal effect was through some restaurants going out of business— and reducing the number of new firms entering to replace them. Those restaurants going out of business were primarily restaurants rated lower in quality. Employment in five-star restaurants was unaffected.[42]

In Seattle as well, the response to a higher local minimum wage rate increase was that a number of restaurants simply closed down.[43] A study published by the National Bureau of Economic Research measured employment by hours of work, as well as by the number of workers employed, and concluded that "the minimum wage ordinance lowered low-wage employees' earnings by an average of $125 per month in 2016."[44] Thus a theoretical increase in income from a higher minimum wage became, in the real world, a significant *decrease* in income.

Another problem with trying to determine the effect of a minimum wage law on unemployment is that the proportion of the work force directly affected by a minimum wage is often small. Therefore unemployment among that fraction of the work force can be swamped by fluctuations in the unemployment rate among the larger number of other employees around them.

This is less of a problem in situations where most of the employees are earning a wage low enough to be directly affected by a minimum wage law. But five-star restaurants were unlikely to be having inexperienced teenagers delivering food to their customers' tables, even if restaurants like McDonald's or Burger King often have teenagers delivering food over the counter to their customers.

Alternative ways of assessing the effect of a minimum wage on unemployment would include gathering data restricted to just the kinds of inexperienced and unskilled workers directly affected, such as teenagers. We have already seen, in Chapter 2, how minimum wage laws affect both teenage unemployment in general and racial disparities in teenage unemployment rates as well.

Yet another way of assessing the effect of minimum wage laws on unemployment would be to gather unemployment data on places and times where there have been no minimum wage laws at all, so that these unemployment rates could be compared to unemployment rates in places and times where there have been minimum wages laws— especially where these have been comparable societies or, ideally, the very same society in the same era, with and without a minimum wage law.

By focusing on teenagers in general, or black teenagers in particular, it is possible to see the effects of minimum wage laws more clearly and precisely, since these are workers on whom such laws have their greatest impact, because these are a population most lacking in education, job skills and experience, and therefore earning especially low wage rates. Moreover, there are extensive statistics on what happened to these populations in the labor markets from the late 1940s to the present.

What is most striking about statistics on American teenage unemployment rates in the late 1940s is that (1) these unemployment rates were only a fraction of the levels of unemployment to which we have become accustomed to seeing in later decades, and (2) there was little or no difference between the unemployment rates of black and white teenagers then.

Internationally, unemployment rates have been markedly lower in times and places where neither governments nor labor unions set most wage rates. Most modern nations have had minimum wage laws, but the few that have not have tended to have strikingly lower unemployment rates. These would include Switzerland and Singapore today and Hong Kong under British rule, prior to the 1997 return of Hong Kong to China. There was also no federal minimum wage law in the United States before the Davis–Bacon Act of 1931, which impacted wage rates in the construction industry.

As for hard data on unemployment rates in these places and times, *The Economist* magazine reported in 2003: "Switzerland's unemployment neared a five-year high of 3.9% in February."[45] But this "high" (for Switzerland) unemployment rate returned to a more normal (for Switzerland) 3.1 percent in later years.[46]

In 2013, Singapore's unemployment rate was 2.1 percent.[47] In 1991, when Hong Kong was still a British colony, it too had no minimum wage law, and its unemployment rate was under 2 percent.[48] In the United States, the last administration with no federal minimum wage law at any time was the Coolidge administration in the 1920s. During President Coolidge's last four years in office, the annual unemployment rate ranged from a high of 4.2 percent to a low of 1.8 percent.[49]

Yet discussions of minimum wage laws, even by academic scholars, are often based on the intentions and presumed effects of these laws, rather than being based on empirical evidence as to their actual consequences.

IMPLICATIONS

On the larger question of statistical errors in general, whether errors of omission or commission, these errors often seem to support a particular social vision. This suggests the possibility that pursuit of a social cause can affect how causation is perceived or presented to others.

Even in the absence of any such concerns, however, the emphasis on complex statistical analysis in economics and other fields— however valuable, or even vital, such statistical analysis may be in many cases— can lead to overlooking simple but fundamental questions as to whether the numbers on which these complex analyses are based are in fact measuring what they seem to be measuring, or claim to be measuring.

"Income" statistics which lump together annual salaries and multi-year capital gains are just one of many sets of statistics which could stand much closer scrutiny at this fundamental level— especially if laws and policies affecting millions of human beings are to be based on statistical conclusions.

More broadly, the validity of numbers in general often depends on the reliability of the *words* describing what those numbers are measuring.

Statistics on tax rates, for example, can be grossly misleading when changes in tax rates are described in such terms as "a $300 billion increase in taxes" or "a $300 billion decrease in taxes."

All that the government can do in reality is change the tax *rate*. How much tax *revenue* that will produce depends on how people react. There have been some times when higher tax rates have produced lower tax revenues, and some other times when lower tax rates have produced higher tax revenues.

In the 1920s, for example, the tax rate on the highest incomes was reduced from 73 percent to 24 percent— and the income tax *revenue* rose substantially— especially tax revenues received from people in the highest income brackets. Under the older and higher tax rate, vast sums of money from wealthy investors were sheltered in tax-exempt securities, such as municipal bonds— an amount estimated to be three times the size of the annual federal budget and more than half as large as the national debt.[50]

Tax-exempt securities tend not to receive as high a rate of return on investments as other securities, whose earnings are taxed. What this meant was that sufficiently lower tax rates made it profitable for wealthy investors to take their money out of tax shelters and invest it in the market economy, where there was a higher rate of earnings, leaving them better off on net balance, even after paying income taxes that they had avoided before.

In terms of *words on paper*, the official tax rate was cut from 73 percent to 24 percent in the 1920s. But, in terms of *events in the real world*, the tax rate actually paid— on staggering sums of money previously hidden in tax shelters— *rose* from zero percent to 24 percent. This produced huge increases in tax revenues received from high-income people, both absolutely and as a percentage of all income taxes collected.[51] That is because 24 percent of something is larger than 73 percent of nothing.

Tax rate cuts in some later administrations also led to increases in tax revenues.[52] For example, a front-page news story in the *New York Times* of July 9, 2006 said: "An unexpectedly steep rise in tax revenues from corporations and the wealthy is driving down the projected budget deficit this year."[53]

However unexpected this increase in tax revenues, after tax rates had been cut, may have been to the *New York Times*, others who had been following economic history would know that this had happened before under administrations of both political parties. But none of these facts has made the slightest difference to those who continue to call tax rate reductions "tax cuts for the rich," even when high-income people end up paying more tax revenue than before. The very possibility that tax rates and tax revenues can move in opposite directions has seldom been mentioned in the media— a crucial error of omission.

Similarly, people who discuss *raising* the government-mandated minimum wage rate talk as if this would automatically mean having the lowest-paid workers' income *rise*, from $10 an hour to $15 per hour, for example. In reality, for millions of inexperienced and unskilled young workers, it can mean that the wages they receive in fact *fall* from $10 an hour to zero, when they are unable to find jobs. Even those who have and keep their jobs can nevertheless end up with lower incomes, as a result of having fewer hours of work available in the wake of a minimum wage increase, as a National Bureau of Economic Research study showed happened in Seattle in 2016, for example.[54]

Statistics matter greatly. But so do the words used to describe those statistics. Unless we are prepared to stop and think beyond the words to the realities, we are all too likely to be manipulated and stampeded by a heady mixture of numbers and rhetoric.

Chapter 5

SOCIAL VISIONS and

HUMAN CONSEQUENCES

M any people may expect discussions of economic and social disparities to end with "solutions"— usually something that the government can create, institutionalize, staff and pay for with the taxpayers' money.

The goal here is entirely different. There has never been a shortage of people eager to draw up blueprints for running other people's lives. But any "solution," however valid as of a given moment under given conditions, is subject to obsolescence at some later time under changed conditions.

The hope here is that clarification is less perishable, and can be applied to both existing issues related to economic and social disparities and to new issues, involving the same subject, that are sure to arise with the passage of time. Given the limitations of prophecy, the point here is to seek to provide enough clarification to enable others to make up their own minds about the inevitable claims and counter-claims sure to arise from those who are promoting their own notions or their own interests.

THE INVINCIBLE FALLACY

At the heart of many discussions of disparities among individuals, groups and nations is the seemingly invincible fallacy that outcomes in human endeavors would be equal, or at least comparable or random, if there were no biased interventions, on the one hand, nor genetic deficiencies, on the other. This preconception, which spans the ideological spectrum, is in utter defiance of both logic and empirical evidence from around the world, and over millennia of recorded history.

As noted in Chapter 1, individual prerequisites for success in various endeavors may be more or less normally distributed, as in a bell curve, but that does *not* mean that the presence of *all* the prerequisites simultaneously will also be normally distributed. Whether among human beings or in nature, highly skewed distributions of outcomes with multiple prerequisites have been common around the world. Nevertheless, the fallacy persists that skewed distributions of income, employment and other social outcomes show either discrimination or genetic deficiencies.

The human species can be divided and subdivided in many ways— by race, sex, age, birth order or by the different geographic settings in which peoples have lived (coastal peoples compared to inland peoples; mountain peoples compared to peoples living in river valleys), and so on. Among all these subdivisions, and others, large disparities in outcomes have been the rule, not the exception.

The real per capita income that Britain reached in 1880 was not reached by Spain until 1960, and by Portugal until 1970— and, at these latter dates, the real per capita income in both Spain and Portugal was not quite half that in contemporary Britain.[1] Homicide rates in Eastern Europe have, for centuries, been some multiple of homicide rates in Western Europe, and homicide rates in different regions of the United States have likewise differed by some multiple.[2]

Yet Britain had no power to suppress the economic development of Spain or Portugal, just as Western Europe had no power to make the homicide rate higher in Eastern Europe. Disparities do not imply discrimination. Nor is discrimination automatically excluded. It is one of many possibilities, each of which has to establish its claims with evidence, rather than being an automatic presumption.

As already noted, even such natural phenomena as earthquakes, lightning and tornadoes likewise show highly skewed distributions around the world, as well as within the same country. Thunderstorms are 20 times as frequent in southern Florida as in coastal California, for example.[3] More than half the geysers in the entire world are in Yellowstone National Park.[4] Asia has more than 70 mountain peaks higher than 20,000 feet, and Africa has none.[5]

The litany of highly skewed outcomes, both among humans and in nature, is almost limitless.[6] Nevertheless, an implicit assumption persists that equal, or at least comparable, outcomes would exist among different groups of people, except for adverse interventions against some, or genetic deficiencies among others.

These are not just theoretical issues. The ramifications impact laws and policies. The Supreme Court of the United States has enshrined the prevailing fallacy in the form of its "disparate impact" standard for presuming discrimination. Yet median age differences among groups, varying by a decade or decades, are alone enough to preclude proportional representation in occupations requiring either long years of experience or the physical vitality of youth— even if all groups were absolutely identical in every other aspect besides age.

Age disparities exist among nations, as among individuals. There are more than twenty nations with median ages in their forties, and more than twenty other nations with median ages under twenty.[7] How rational is it to expect nations with such large and consequential differences in adult experience to have equal, or even comparable, economic productivity? And among nations, as among individuals, age differences are just one difference among many.

Seekers of "social justice," in the sense of equal or comparable outcomes, proceed as if eliminating racial, sex or other group discriminations would produce some approximation of that ideal. But what of the implications of the fact that a majority of the people in American prisons were raised with either one parent or no parent?[8] This does not even get into the *qualitative* dimension of parenting, though we know that educational differences among parents have been correlated with differences in educational and career outcomes among their children, even when those offspring were men who were all in the top one percent in IQs.[9]

Sometimes just a single inconspicuous difference in circumstances can make a huge, historic difference in human outcomes. One of the monumental natural catastrophes of the nineteenth century was the famine in Ireland that was due to the failure of the potato crop, at a time when potatoes were the principal food of the Irish. Deaths by starvation and by diseases related to malnutrition are estimated to have claimed a million lives in Ireland, a country of only 8.5 million people at the time.[10]

Nearly two million people are estimated to have fled that famine-stricken country between the mid-1840s and the mid-1850s[11]— altogether a massive loss of population in a small country. Yet the very same kind of potato was grown in the United States— where Ireland's potatoes originated— with no crop failure.

The source of that crop failure has been traced to a fertilizer used in planting potatoes on both sides of the Atlantic. That fertilizer contained a fungus which flourished in the mild and moist climate of Ireland, but not in the hot and dry summers of Idaho and other potato-growing areas of the United States.[12] That one difference meant millions of human tragedies and a massive loss of population from which Ireland did not recover, until generations later.

Morally neutral factors such as crop failures, birth order, geographic settings, technological advances, or demographic and cultural differences are among the many reasons why economic and social outcomes so often fail to fit the preconception of equal or comparable results.

Yet morally neutral factors seem to attract far less attention than other causal factors which stir moral outrage, such as discrimination or exploitation. But our emotional responses tell us nothing about the *causal* weight of different factors, however much those emotional responses may shape political crusades and government policies. But which causal factors predominate at a given place or time is ultimately an empirical question, independent of our emotions or inclinations.

Those who seem to be promising an end to existing disparities as a result of whatever policies they advocate, may be promising what cannot be delivered, regardless of the particular policies being advocated. Moreover, the clash between numerical goals, fervently pursued, and the repeatedly frustrated attempts to reach those goals is not without social consequences, including dire consequences for society as a whole— and perhaps especially dire for the less fortunate, who suffer most when social order breaks down amid heady crusades.

This is not to say that all attempts to help lagging individuals or groups are futile. On the contrary, many dramatic rises from poverty to prosperity, and even rises to the forefront of human achievements, have occurred at various times in countries around the world. But seldom, if ever, has this been a result of policies based on the fallacy of assuming equal outcomes in the absence of group discrimination or on the basis of an assumption of a fictitious sameness among peoples.

The actual consequences of the prevailing social vision of our times cannot be assessed on the basis of its good intentions or even its plausibility. The real test is what has happened when it has been applied, and what the implications are of the social consequences.

Educational Implications

Among the institutions where the prevailing fallacy takes a painfully sweeping toll are those low-income and minority schools in America (and low-income white schools in England) where young thugs are allowed to destroy the education— and the futures— of other students there, by making those other students and their teachers targets of daily disruptions, harassments, threats and violence.[13]

In the United States, federal agencies have pressured and threatened schools where statistics show a disciplining of black male students at rates that are disproportionate to the disciplining of other students. The invincible fallacy in the background trumps the most blatant and disastrous realities right in front of our eyes.

Even aside from any questions about differences in capabilities or potentialities, there are inescapable differences in what people *want* to do. Does anyone seriously believe that Asian American youngsters have as much interest in playing basketball as black youngsters have? Or does anyone doubt that the Asian youngsters' lesser interest in basketball may have something to do with the dearth of Asian Americans among professional basketball players?

Differences in what individuals and groups *want* to do, and are prepared to prioritize, are too often ignored in many well-intentioned policies. The "no child left behind" educational policies, for example, introduced during the administration of President George W. Bush, ignored the painful possibility that there was no such universal desire for education as implicitly assumed, and that *some* uninterested children's behavior prevented *other* children from learning. Given these ignored realities, the disruptive or violent children must be separated from others, if those others are to have a decent chance for a decent education.

Moreover, the need to separate the disruptive and violent children is independent of whether or not there is any "solution" currently available, or on the horizon, for changing the behavior of disruptive and/or violent children. The alternative is to sacrifice the education of unending generations of poor and minority children until such indefinite time as a "solution" for misbehaving or violent classmates can be found.

The extraordinary educational successes of some chains of charter schools in low-income, minority neighborhoods[14] may well be due, at least in part, to the self-sorting of families in those neighborhoods who care enough about better education for their own children to enter the lotteries by which applicants are chosen for admission to charter schools.

In short, disruptive and violent children are "left behind" in the public schools, the Bush administration approach notwithstanding. This is one of those "second-best" options, when the first best option— punishing and/or explicitly isolating disruptive and violent students from all other students— is precluded for political or ideological reasons.

Nor is this problem peculiar to the United States. There are some schools in England where classrooms have been described as being "on the knife-edge of anarchy most of the time."[15] In both countries, one-sixth of the children are functionally illiterate.[16] This is a painful waste of mental potential, and the poor can afford it least of all.

More generally, government programs to transfer people *en masse* from bad environments to better environments, in order to improve their prospects in life, ignore vast amounts of empirical evidence that this simply does not work on any scale commensurate with its negative consequences to people into whose midst they are thrust. Moreover, those who promote such programs usually refuse to consider the possibility— even as a testable hypothesis— that it is precisely the presence of people with bad behavior patterns that makes bad environments bad, and a dearth of such people elsewhere that makes better environments better.

Political Implications

The most spectacularly successful political doctrine that swept into power in countries around the world in the twentieth century was Marxism, based on the implicit presumption that differences in wealth were due to capitalists growing rich by keeping the workers poor, through "exploitation."

This version of the invincible fallacy apparently seemed plausible to people in many different countries and cultures. But, if the wealth of rich capitalists comes from exploitation of poor workers, then we might expect to find that where there are larger concentrations of rich capitalists, we would find correspondingly larger concentrations of poverty.

But the hard facts point in the opposite direction. The United States has more than five times as many billionaires as Africa and the Middle East put together,[17] yet most Americans— including those living below the official poverty line— have a far higher standard of living than that of the populations of Africa and the Middle East. It would be difficult to find even a single country, ruled by Marxists, where the standard of living of working-class people has been as high as that of working-class people in a number of capitalist countries.

This is despite the fact that the first and largest of the avowedly Marxist countries, the Soviet Union, was one of the most richly endowed nations in the world, when it came to natural resources, if not *the* most richly endowed.[18] Yet the standard of living of ordinary people in the Soviet Union was nowhere close to the average standard of living of ordinary people in most of Western Europe, or in the United States or Australia. But here, as elsewhere, hard facts have been repeatedly trumped by heady visions, such as that presented in *The Communist Manifesto*.

Other, non-Marxist, doctrines have been built on the same foundation of assumptions, and they too have had their sweeping political triumphs in the twentieth century, usually in the form of expansive welfare states in the second half of that century, with the 1960s being their pivotal, triumphant decade.

Hypothesis-testing has usually played a remarkably small role in these intellectual, legal and political developments. Indeed, scholars who have tested prevailing views against hard data, and found the prevailing views lacking, have often encountered hostility and demonization rather than counter-evidence.[19] Riots to prevent their speaking have disgraced many of the most prestigious academic campuses in the United States— indeed, especially such campuses.[20]

Social Implications

If these were simply intra-mural contests among the intelligentsia, there would be little reason for others to be concerned about them. But social visions, and even the very catchwords and verbal style in which those visions are discussed, diffuse far beyond those who create and elaborate social visions.

When treating imprisoned murderers in England, for example, physician Theodore Dalrymple found them using the same passive voice sentence constructions found among the intelligentsia when discussing social pathologies. Murderers discussing their crimes say such things as, "the knife went in," instead of saying that they stabbed their victim.[21]

An echo of elite intellectuals even appeared in an old musical, *West Side Story*, where a character says, "Hey, I'm depraved on account I'm deprived." Intellectuals say it more sophisticatedly, but they are nevertheless saying essentially the same thing. While what they are saying might be a plausible hypothesis to be tested empirically, it is too often treated as an established fact, requiring no such testing.

Yet neither in England nor in the United States was such depravity as rampant violence and other social pathology as common among low-income people in the first half of the twentieth century, when they were more deprived, as in the second half, when the welfare state made them better off in material terms.

The importance of social visions goes far beyond the rhetoric they spawn. In a democratic nation, there can be no welfare state without a social vision first prevailing politically, a vision justifying the creation or expansion of a welfare state. Moreover, the triumph of that vision in Western societies during the 1960s entailed far more than the welfare state itself.

With the prevailing social vision came a more non-judgmental approach to behavior, as well as multiculturalism, a de-emphasis of policing and punishments, and an emphasis on demographically based "fair shares" for all.

The reasons for all these beliefs were elaborated in many ways by many individuals and groups. What has been elaborated far less often are empirical tests as to the validity of those hypotheses, in terms of the results expected from following this vision, versus what actually happened.

It is not simply that the social vision which greatly expanded the welfare state and undermined traditional moral values failed to achieve all its goals and fostered some negative consequences. What is particularly salient is that various social pathologies which had been declining— some for years, decades or even centuries— had a sudden resurgence, as these new and often self-congratulatory ideas triumphed politically and socially in the 1960s, on both sides of the Atlantic.

In the United States, murder rates, rates of infection with venereal diseases and rates of teenage pregnancies were among these social pathologies whose steep declines were suddenly reversed in the 1960s, as all these pathologies soared to new and tragic heights.[22] After decades of declining murder rates in the United States, that rate by 1960 was just under half of what it had been in the mid-1930s.[23] But the murder rate reversed and doubled from 1960 to 1980,[24] in the wake of new legal restrictions on law enforcement, in keeping with the new social vision.

These trends, and reversals of trends, were not peculiar to the United States. A monumental treatise on the decline of violence in the world over the centuries— *The Better Angels of Our Nature* by Steven Pinker— pointed out that, in Europe, "rates of violence did a U-turn in the 1960s," including "a bounce in homicide rates that brought them back to levels they had said goodbye to a century before."[25]

Perhaps the most striking— and most alarming— increases in violence and disorder were in places long known for law-abiding, orderly and polite behavior, England being a preeminent example.

American economist J.K. Galbraith happened to be in London in May 1945, when a crowd estimated at "two or three hundred thousand"— and mostly young people— was gathered to celebrate the end of the war in Europe. He wrote to his wife: "Like all British crowds it was most orderly."[26]

In sports competition, British competitors were renowned for their sportsmanship. In a 1953 soccer match, for example, the team leading, with only two minutes to go, saw an opposing player snatch victory from them with only seconds left in the game— and members of the losing team stood up and applauded him. But, by the mid-1960s, such sportsmanship was gone, even in Britain's classic sportsmanlike game, cricket. Vulgar insults were now common among British players, and among players in British offshoot societies Australia and New Zealand.[27]

The same social degeneration affected law-abiding behavior, during the same era. London had a total of just 12 armed robberies all year in 1954, at a time when anyone could buy a shotgun. But, in later years, armed robberies rose to 1,400 by 1981 and 1,600 in 1991,[28] despite increasingly severe restrictions on the purchase of firearms. As for orderly crowds, in 2011 urban riots spread through London, Manchester and other British cities, involving thousands of hoodlums and looters who set fire to homes and businesses, as well as beating and robbing people on the streets and throwing gasoline bombs at police cars.[29]

The coarsening of life took other forms in England, during the era of the new social vision. It was not uncommon for men found unconscious on the streets, and taken to hospitals where the medical staff worked to restore their health, to later speak insultingly and abusively to those who had cared for them. Insults and abuse of medical personnel became sufficiently widespread that the National Health Service posted signs in its facilities, warning that abusive and threatening behavior toward the staff would be prosecuted.[30]

Other social pathologies, which had existed before, expanded to new magnitudes. These included fatherless children and urban riots. As of 1960, two-thirds of all black American children were living with both parents. That declined over the years, until only *one-third* were living with both parents in 1995. Fifty-two percent were living with their mother, 4 percent with their father and 11 percent with neither.[31] Among black families in poverty, 85 percent of the children had no father present.[32]

Although white families did not have nearly as high a proportion of children living with one parent as blacks had in 1960, nevertheless the 1960s marked a sharp upturn in white children born to unwed mothers, to levels several times what they had been in the decades preceding the 1960s. By 2008, nearly 30 percent of white children were born to unwed mothers. Among white women with less than 12 years of education, more than 60 percent of their children were born to unwed mothers in the first decade of the twenty-first century.[33]

These social patterns were not peculiar to the United States, but were common in a number of Western societies. In England and Wales, for example, 44 percent of children were born to unwed mothers in 2007. Other countries where more than 40 percent of children were born to unwed mothers included France, Sweden, Norway, Denmark and Iceland. In most of these countries, this represented a major increase just since 1980.[34]

Urban riots in America, which had been sporadic in earlier years, spread in massive waves from coast to coast during the 1960s. Educational standards and performances in American schools began a decades' long decline in the 1960s, whether measured by test scores, by professors' assessments of incoming college students, by students' own reports of their time spent studying, or by employers' complaints about a lack of basic skills among the young people they hired.[35]

The factors on which those with the prevailing social vision relied for educational success— more spending for education in general and racial integration for blacks in particular— proved to be of little or no effectiveness.

Seldom does any era in human history have exclusively negative or exclusively positive trends. Perhaps the most often cited positive achievements of the 1960s in the United States were the civil rights laws and policies that put an end to racially discriminatory laws and policies in the South, especially the Civil Rights Act of 1964 and the Voting Rights Act of 1965.

Although this has often been credited to the social vision of the political left, in reality a higher percentage of Congressional Republicans than of Congressional Democrats voted for these landmark laws.[36] But facts that do not fit the prevailing vision tend to be simply ignored.

Much of the social retrogression that took place on both sides of the Atlantic is traceable to the central tenet of the prevailing social vision, that unequal outcomes are due to adverse treatment of the less fortunate. This preconception became a fount of grievance-driven attitudes, emotions and actions— including what has been aptly called "decivilizing" behavior in many contexts.[37]

Despite what was, at best, a mixed record of outcomes from the new social vision, and the new laws and policies that flowed from that vision, the image of the 1960s has been celebrated in the media, in politics and in academia, especially by those who took part in its social crusades. The response of one of the high-level participants in the 1960s crusades, upon meeting best-selling author Shelby Steele, who had expressed some skepticism about that era, was not atypical:

> "Look," he said irritably, "*only*— and I mean *only*— the government can get to that kind of poverty, that entrenched, deep poverty. And I don't care what you say. If this country was decent, it would let the government try again."[38]

Shelby Steele's attempt to focus on facts about the actual consequences of various government programs of the 1960s brought a heated response:

> "Damn it, we *saved* this country!" he all but shouted. "This country was about to blow up. There were riots everywhere. You can stand there now in hindsight and criticize, but we had to keep the country together, my friend."[39]

That a high official of the Lyndon Johnson administration of the 1960s could believe things so completely counter to demonstrable facts was one sign of the power of a vision.

His claim that only government programs could effectively deal with deep poverty was contradicted by the plain fact that the black poverty rate declined from 87 percent in 1940 to 47 percent in 1960,[40] *prior* to the great expansion of the welfare state that began in the 1960s under the Johnson administration. There was a far more modest decline in the poverty rate among blacks after the Johnson administration's massive "war on poverty" programs began.

As for ghetto riots, these were never as numerous, nor of such magnitudes of violence, in the 1940s and 1950s, as they became in the 1960s, when the social vision behind the welfare state became triumphant in politics, in educational institutions and in the media. Nor were there similar numbers or magnitudes of violence in riots in the 1980s, during the eight years of the Reagan administration, in which that social vision was repudiated.

Much more is involved here than incorrect inferences from demonstrable facts by one man. This was a far too common example of the ability of a social vision to not only survive, but thrive, in defiance of empirical evidence.

"SOLUTIONS"

No one who looks at the facts of life can look very far without encountering not only extreme disparities in outcomes but also the pervasive reality of luck. Some may think of luck in terms of being born rich or poor, black or white, or any number of other social distinctions. But luck extends far beyond such conventional social categories, right down to the individual level.

No one can choose what kinds of parents to have, or whether to be the first born or the last born in a family, much less what kind of surrounding community, with what kind of culture, to grow up in. Yet such wholly fortuitous factors, from the standpoint of the individual, can have a major influence on how one's life turns out.

As already noted, a study of American prison inmates found that most were raised either by a single parent (43 percent) or raised with neither parent present (14 percent).[41] It was pointed out elsewhere that those children who had a parent who was imprisoned ended up in prison themselves several times more often than members of the general population.[42] Similarly, in Britain, a study found that 27 percent of prison inmates had been placed in protective child custody at some point while growing up.[43]

If we have no control over luck, and no control over the past, then it is all the more important that we concentrate on those things over which we can at least hope to have some influence— notably providing incentives affecting future behavior.

Income is an obvious incentive and, because it is an incentive affecting economic behavior at all levels, we cannot treat incomes as if they were just numbers that we can change to suit our wishes, without considering how that will change behavior and the economic consequences that follow from behavior. Such consequences of changed behavior affect the output on which the standard of living of a whole society depends.

Nor are those economic consequences something that we can conjure up from our imaginations, or deduce from our preconceptions. The hard facts of history can tell us something and current factual tests of our hypotheses can tell us more.

The same is true of incentives affecting crime, including both law enforcement and punishment. Here, perhaps even more so than with economic issues and incentives, utter ignorance of relevant facts seldom seems to inhibit sweeping and passionate conclusions.

Many people who have never encountered the kinds of dangers inherent in law enforcement do not hesitate to say that "excessive force" was used against someone resisting arrest or even someone threatening the police. People who have never fired a gun in their lives likewise do not hesitate to express shock and anger that "so many" bullets were fired in an encounter with a criminal.*

Even when an overwhelming force of police arrive on a threatening scene, bringing the threat to a complete halt without using any force at all, critics

---

* On a personal note, as someone who was once a pistol coach in the Marine Corps, I have not been surprised at all that large numbers of shots were fired in such situations.

often call that "over-reaction" to the threat, which never reached dangerous levels. The possibility that it never reached dangerous levels precisely because of an overwhelming police presence never seems to occur to such critics.

As regards punishment, a criminal's unhappy childhood cannot be changed, and whether the person he has become can be changed is by no means a foregone conclusion. Nor are the dangers he represents to other people's safety, or their lives, dangers that can be banished by saying soothing words like "rehabilitation" or "alternatives to incarceration."

This is not simply a matter of our choices, but of our inherent limitations. What we might choose to do if we were omniscient is no guide at all to the painfully limited choices we may have when we are very far short of omniscience— and when negative "unintended consequences" have become so common as to become a cliché.

If and when "rehabilitation" gets beyond being a word and becomes a demonstrable fact that can be relied on in the future, then its benefits can be weighed against its costs, like anything else. These costs include the inevitable failures that go with any human endeavor, and the costs of such failures extend beyond economic resources to lives lost.

As for good luck, that too is part of the irrevocable past. But awareness of the role of luck might temper the arrogance of some who have been successful, and temper the resentments of others who have been unsuccessful, and who seek bogeymen to blame for their condition— bogeymen who can be readily supplied by politicians, "leaders," activists and the media.

Since there is nothing easier to find than sins among human beings, individuals can always be found who have said and done bad things— and can thus be more or less automatically blamed for the bad outcomes of others. Beyond that, there is always the fundamental fallacy that outcomes would be equal or comparable in the absence of malign actions against the less fortunate.

Here as elsewhere, the only times over which we can reasonably hope to have any influence are the present and the future. The most we can do with the past is to learn from it.

Efforts can be made to reduce the number of people currently likely to have damaging childhoods, but the outcomes of such efforts depend not simply on how fervently we wish for better results, but on our knowledge, resources and wisdom— none of which is available in unlimited supply, and deficiencies in which can lead not merely to failure but even to counterproductive outcomes, extending to major social disasters.

At the societal level, the same severe and painful limitations apply when seeking to redress the wrongs of the past. Where the deaths of both the victims and the victimizers put them completely beyond our power, our frustration cannot justify making symbolic restitution among the living, when the costs of such attempts around the world have been written in blood across the pages of history.

After territorial irredentism has led nations to slaughter each other's people over land that might have little or no value in itself, simply because it once belonged in a different political jurisdiction, at a time beyond any living person's memory, what is to be expected from instilling the idea of *social* irredentism, growing out of historic wrongs done to other people?

Such wrongs abound in times and places around the world— inflicted on, and perpetrated by, people of every race, creed and color. But what can any society today hope to gain by having newborn babies in that society enter the world as heirs to prepackaged grievances against other babies born into that same society on the same day?

Individual "Solutions"

Many people, recognizing that those less fortunate may not have had the same opportunities as themselves, have tended to be less demanding about the standards being applied, especially as regards qualities not developed as well within the culture in which the less fortunate have grown up. A promising youngster, with many good qualities and strong potentialities, may not yet have acquired the habit of punctuality, for example. A generous inclination might be not to make a fuss over a chronic tendency of that youngster to arrive 10 or 15 minutes late.

Perhaps a case can be made for modifying the tone or manner in which such a person is penalized for tardiness. But that is very different from saying that a lack of punctuality can be ignored, or penalized less, than with someone from a more fortunate culture, who has been trained from an early age to be on time. Once again, that is part of the past that we can do nothing about, while the future consequences of what we do in the present are our real responsibility.

In view of the fact that the kinds of future endeavors to which a promising young person with many good qualities can aspire are likely to have multiple prerequisites, and that the absence of just one of those prerequisites can negate the presence of all the others, a decision to ignore a deficiency in one of those prerequisites may not be an act of kindness, in terms of its effects on that youngster's future prospects.

The higher a promising young person goes occupationally, the more high-level people are likely to be encountered in the future— people for whom time is money, and who cannot be kept waiting repeatedly, without adverse consequences to that tardy young person's future.

Similarly, loosening behavioral standards in general for a child who has grown up without any consistent structure of discipline, at home or in school, risks having whatever abilities or potentialities that child has be rendered futile in a sweeping range of future endeavors with multiple prerequisites that will be encountered in adulthood, if not before.

Being "understanding" or "non-judgmental" toward a young person from a culturally limited background may seem humane, but it can be the kiss of death, as far as that individual's future is concerned. Something as simple as whether or not one speaks standard English can open or close doors of opportunity— again, especially in higher levels of achievement in many fields. Yet there are educators who see an emphasis on standard English as needless cultural narrowness, if not racism.

Linguistic scholar John McWhorter, for example, sprang to the defense of those in ghetto schools who want to use "black English" in teaching black youngsters. Professor McWhorter contrasted "the general American take on the matter" as one seeing blacks as using "a lot of slang and bad grammar"[44] with the way linguistic scholars judge languages.

By the latter criterion, he depicts "black English" as being as much of a coherent language as French, Arabic or Chinese, all of which have colloquial versions different from their formal versions.[45] As for why many Americans look at "black English" in the negative way they do, McWhorter says: "Certainly, racism is part of the answer,"[46] even if "the racist element in all this vitriol" is not the whole story.[47]

Professor McWhorter sided with those educators who said that "black English" can be used in schools "as an aid to imparting Standard English to black kids." Like variations on other languages, he depicts "black English" as something that people speak "in addition to" standard English, and it functions as a *lingua franca*, according to the sub-title of his book.[48]

This picture of youngsters in the ghetto as simply being bilingual differs painfully from the reality of their abysmal scores on tests of English. Far from being a *lingua franca* facilitating intergroup communication, as John McWhorter depicts it, "black English" is a *barrier* to communication with hundreds of millions of Americans, as well as a barrier to communication with half a billion people around the world who speak English.

It is a devastating constriction of the future opportunities available to black youngsters themselves. Where are the books on mathematics, science, engineering, medicine and innumerable other subjects that are written in "black English"? Professor McWhorter's defiant posture of defending fellow blacks and their way of talking[49] contrasts painfully with the social reality of sacrificing the futures of whole generations of young blacks.

Language issues are not peculiar to blacks or to the United States. Such issues have polarized societies around the world, sometimes to the point of riots and terrorism, as in India, or even a decades-long civil war, as in Sri Lanka.

Because languages in Western Europe developed written versions centuries earlier than the languages of Eastern Europe, the range of written material in the Slavic languages was far more limited, in centuries past, than the range of written material in Western European languages. Thus a Czech child in the Habsburg Empire during the early nineteenth century could be taught in his own native language only in elementary school. It was 1848 before there were high schools teaching in the Czech language.[50]

Prior to that time, a Czech youngster had to learn German, in order to become educated above the elementary school level, and thus be able to aspire to a wider range of occupational opportunities as an adult. None of this had anything to do with the linguistic characteristics of either the German language or the Czech language, and everything to do with the inherent constraints of the time, when the prerequisite written knowledge for some professions was available in German but not yet in Czech.

Ironically, a Japanese-owned multinational company has decreed that English will be the sole language of the enterprise, wherever the company's branches are located around the world.[51] In other words, they recognize that English is the *lingua franca* of international commerce, as it is the language of international airline pilots communicating with airports around the world.

In Singapore, with an overwhelmingly Asian population, not only are all school children required to learn English, the language of instruction in other subjects is conducted in English.[52] In such cases, the choice of language is based on practical considerations for the welfare of people, rather than on symbolic or ideological issues.

Practical issues about social and economic realities, seldom have anything to do with the kinds of things that preoccupy academic linguists. Group spokesmen, activists or "leaders" may be preoccupied with languages as badges of cultural identity, but cultures exist to serve human beings. Human beings do not exist to preserve cultures, or to preserve a socially isolated constituency for the benefit of "leaders."

Government "Solutions"

"Solutions" can be a society's biggest problem— and especially governmental "solutions"— because government is essentially a categorical institution in an incremental world. When many desirable things compete for a share of inherently limited resources, individuals making decisions for themselves can make incremental trade-offs, giving up a certain amount of X to get a certain amount of Y— and at some point putting a stop to that particular trade-off, when they feel a need to conserve their dwindling supply of X and are approaching a more adequate supply of Y.

Government decisions, however, tend to be categorical: Things are either legal or illegal, and people are either eligible or ineligible for benefits provided by government.

Billionaires are legally eligible for government subsidies in agriculture, even if there is not enough money to provide adequate medical care in government hospitals for military veterans. Government employees are eligible for pensions that pay far more generously than comparable workers receive in the private sector, even when there is not enough money to repair and maintain the safety of crumbling infrastructure.

Categorical decision-making also means that words can carry more weight than realities. "Poverty" means whatever government statisticians say it means, so that a scholar who had spent years studying economic conditions in Latin America could say, "the poverty line in the United States is the upper-middle class in Mexico."[53] But another scholar, taking words more literally, could lament that America's poor were "having difficulty keeping food on the table."[54] How people with difficulty keeping food on the table can be overweight, even more often than other Americans,[55] is a mystery he did not explain. Words trumped realities.

More important than the assessments of intellectuals are the institutional characteristics of government. As a categorical institution, government can deal with things that we categorically do not want, such as murder, or which we categorically *do* want, such as protection from military attacks by foreign countries. But decisions and actions requiring more finely detailed knowledge for making nuanced incremental adjustments, are often better handled by decision-making processes with more intimate knowledge and involvement— and especially more compelling *feedback* from the actual consequences of the decisions made.

Given how prone *all* human beings are to mistakes, in all kinds of institutions, one of the most important characteristics of any decision-making process is its ability to recognize and correct its own mistakes. Businesses that do not recognize their own mistakes, and change course in time, can face bankruptcy, even when they have been very successful in the past. Individuals suffering the painful consequences of their own bad decisions have often been forced to change course in order to avoid impending catastrophe, and in many cases have ended up with greater personal fulfillment and insight going forward.

Various governmental institutions, however, have major built-in barriers to changing course in response to feedback. For an elected official to admit to having made a mistaken decision, from which millions of voters are suffering, is to face the prospect of the end of a whole career in disgrace. Courts of law are bound by legal precedents, which cannot be reversed willy-nilly without disrupting the effectiveness of the whole framework of law.

Housing "Solutions"

Once government housing programs have been created to help "low-income" families, then any family that meets a government agency's arbitrary definition of "low-income" can receive benefits paid for with the taxpayers' money. In 2017, for example, families of four people each, with a family income of $100,000, were classified as "low-income" families in San Francisco,[56] where housing costs are unusually high.

Why a family's decision to live in expensive San Francisco should be subsidized by the taxpayers— including taxpayers with family incomes under $100,000— is a question that does not even arise in this context, where words with arbitrary meanings and categorical consequences guide government decisions.*

The sorting and unsorting of neighborhoods by ethnicity or income is an example of something which can be done either by government programs or by private market processes, such as those which changed Harlem from a white, middle-class area of Manhattan into a black, working-class area in the early twentieth century. But these different processes operate under different incentives and constraints, leading to very different end results.

---

* Such arbitrary uses of words are not unique to the United States. In Greece, people in "arduous" occupations are legally entitled to retire early on pensions— as early as 55 years old for men and 50 years old for women. Among the occupations designated as "arduous" are hairdressers, radio announcers, waiters and musicians. James Bartholomew, *The Welfare of Nations* (Washington: Cato Institute, 2016), p. 218.

A demographic study of Harlem, as it existed in 1937, showed that the black population had expanded outward from its earlier beginnings at 135th Street and Seventh Avenue, in more or less concentric circles, each circle differing in the proportion of blacks in that circle's total population, and differing also in the social composition of those particular black people from one circle to another.[57] In short, these settlements were not random. People had sorted themselves out, as other people do in countries around the world.

In this study of Harlem, much as in his earlier doctoral dissertation on the black community in Chicago, Professor E. Franklin Frazier found substantial differences in the socioeconomic circumstances in the different concentric circles radiating out from the initial black settlement in Harlem, as the total population of blacks in Harlem increased greatly during the mass migrations from the South.

Blacks were 99 percent of the population in the innermost circle in 1930 and 88 percent of the population in the next circle, but only 6 percent in the outermost fifth circle. Within the black population, Professor Frazier pointed out the "tendency on the part of family groups to move toward the periphery of the community." The proportion of children under the age of five in the population ranged from just under 4 percent in the innermost circle to just over 12 percent in the outermost circle. The proportion of families on welfare in the innermost zone was two and half times the proportion in the outermost zone.[58]

What this meant, both in New York and Chicago, was that those blacks who were most acculturated to the social norms of the larger society led the expansion of the black community into adjoining white communities. There was resistance, even so, but the expansion did continue. By contrast, government programs in later years, aimed at racially and socioeconomically unsorting neighborhoods, have moved blacks from crime-ridden public housing projects into middle-class neighborhoods— both black and white middle-class neighborhoods— and have encountered bitter opposition from pre-existing residents in both cases.

It is not obvious how we can even define a "solution" in a situation where people in three different groups are each seeking to have a better life, when their ways of life clash, unless one arbitrarily assumes that some group's desires automatically override any other group's desires. In short, there are no real "solutions" in such situations, and the best we can reasonably hope for is a viable trade-off.

What actually happens often are especially bitter complaints by middle-class blacks who have sacrificed economically, sometimes for years, in order to be able to afford to move their families away from the kinds of dysfunctional and dangerous ghetto neighbors whom the government now chooses to place in their midst in their new surroundings. But protests from pre-existing residents are often ignored, and those protesting depicted as unworthy people obstructing progress. The alternative is to admit to having imposed a mistaken policy with dire consequences, which could be politically fatal to the promoters of such policies.

Educational "Solutions"

A categorical institution like government cannot be expected to make the best incremental trade-offs. History suggests that government cannot do so, especially when operating within the confines of a social vision based on assumptions of sameness, or at least comparability, among people, when there is no such sameness or comparability even within an underclass minority community in the United States, much less between an underclass minority community and middle-class communities of either minority or majority population.

What can be seen from history, however, is that when people sort themselves out, instead of having the government do so, they seem to get better results— not without strife, but with less strife than in later times when government "solutions" abounded, and so did racial polarization.

This was especially apparent during the years when mandatory busing of school children was imposed, in order to get racial "integration" in schools, for its supposed educational benefits, which largely failed to materialize. However, when low-income minority parents have had a choice of where to send their own children to school, the educational results have been demonstrably— and often dramatically— better in the more successful charter schools.

But charter schools have never attracted the same crusading zeal as the busing campaign, not even when children in ghetto charter schools score above the 90th percentile in math and English, while other children from the same neighborhoods in the regular public schools score below the 10th percentile. Often these radically different educational outcomes have occurred in the very same building, housing both the local neighborhood public school and the local neighborhood charter school serving the same population.

Income and Wealth Redistribution "Solutions"

If those who are more fortunate are the reason others are less fortunate, then such things as redistributing income or wealth may seem much more plausible as a "solution" than in a world where the accumulation of human capital is more fundamental than the accumulation of physical wealth, even though the latter can be measured statistically and confiscated politically. Physical wealth can be confiscated and redistributed in a variety of ways, but human capital cannot be, since it is inside the heads of other people.

In many times and places, various prosperous peoples with much human capital have either fled persecution or have been expelled from the countries where they lived— and in both cases forced to leave behind most of their physical wealth, therefore arriving destitute in some new country.

This was the fate of many Jews expelled from Spain in the fifteenth century, many Huguenots fleeing France in the seventeenth century, and the fate of many Gujaratis expelled from Uganda and Cubans fleeing Communist Cuba in the twentieth century, among many others in other countries around the world in other times.

The fate of the Gujaratis and the Cuban refugees in the twentieth century has been particularly well documented. Many Gujaratis arrived destitute in Britain, but eventually rose again to prosperity. Meanwhile, the Ugandan economy they left behind collapsed, in the absence of others with the same human capital as the Gujaratis.[59]

Cuban refugees likewise rose from their initial poverty on arrival in the United States and, 40 years after their arrival, the total revenue of Cuban-

American businesses was greater than the total revenue of the nation of Cuba.[60]

Something similar happened in the seventeenth century, when large numbers of Huguenots fled religious persecution in France. They took with them skills that had contributed to France's having been a leading— if not *the* leading— economic nation in Europe.

Those skills brought by the Huguenot refugees enabled other countries to produce goods they had previously bought from France, and to compete with France in international markets. The French economy suffered many setbacks in the succeeding decades following the exodus of many Huguenots.[61]

Despite all the voluminous writings making an intellectual or moral case for a confiscation of income and wealth, in the name of "social justice," there has been remarkably little attention paid to the question of the extent to which this can actually be done in any comprehensive, long-run sense. In the short run, confiscation can easily be done, whether by governments or by mobs looting stores. Detroit has been a classic example of both— and of the long-run consequences.[62]

Nevertheless, killing the goose that lays the golden egg is a viable strategy from a purely political standpoint, provided the goose does not die before the next election. A two-decades-long career for one man as mayor of Detroit, from 1974 to 1994, was made possible by policies which drove the most economically productive people out of Detroit, ensuring the mayor's consecutive reelections by the departure of those people most likely to vote against him. It also ensured the decline of Detroit.

Nor was Detroit unique. Such a combination of political success, along with economic and social disaster, can be found in a number of American cities where one political party has stayed in power for decades through redistributionist policies which drove out people who had much human capital, and left the city a hollow shell of its former self, after those tax-paying and job-creating people were gone. Third World nations that have had major confiscations of tangible wealth— whether the capital of foreign investors ("nationalization" of industries) or domestic entrepreneurs— have often suffered a similar fate for similar reasons.

THE PAST AND THE FUTURE

Looking back at the past, there is much to inspire and much to appall. As for the future, all that we can be certain of is that it is coming, whether we are well-prepared or ill-prepared for it.

Perhaps the most heartening things about the past are the innumerable examples of whole peoples who lagged far behind their contemporaries at a given time and yet, in later times, overtook them and moved to the forefront of human achievements.

These would include Britons in the ancient world, when they were an illiterate tribal people, while the ancient Greeks and Romans were laying the intellectual and material foundations of Western civilization— and yet, more than a millennium later, it was the Britons who led the world into the industrial revolution, and established an empire which included one-fourth of the land area in the world and one-fourth of all the human beings on Earth.

At various times and places, China and the Islamic world were more advanced than Europe, and later fell behind, while Japan rose from poverty and backwardness in the middle of the nineteenth century to the forefront of economic and technological achievements in the twentieth century. Jews, who had played little or no role in the revolutionary emergence of science and technology in the early modern era, later produced a wholly disproportionate share of all the scientists who won Nobel Prizes in the twentieth century.

Among the appalling things about the past, it is hard to know which was the worst, since there are all too many candidates, from around the world, for that designation. That something like the Holocaust could have happened, after thousands of years of civilization, and in one of the most advanced societies, is almost as incomprehensible intellectually as it is devastating morally and in terms of showing what depths of depravity are possible in *all* human beings. It is a painful reminder of a description of civilization as "a thin crust over a volcano."

If longevity and universality are criteria, then slavery must be among the leading candidates for the most appalling of all human institutions, for it existed on every inhabited continent for thousands of years, as far back as the history of the human species goes. Yet its full scope is often grossly underestimated today, when slavery is so often discussed as if it were confined to one race enslaving another race, when in fact slavery existed virtually wherever it was feasible for some human beings to enslave other human beings— including in many, if not most, cases people of their own race.[63]

Europeans enslaved other Europeans for centuries before Europeans brought the first African slaves— purchased from other Africans who had enslaved them— to the Western Hemisphere. Nor was it unknown for Europeans to be enslaved by non-Europeans. Just one example were the European slaves brought to the coast of North Africa by pirates. These European slaves were more numerous than the African slaves brought to the United States and to the American colonies from which it was formed.[64] But the politicization of history has shrunk the public perception of slavery to whatever is most expedient for promoting politically correct agendas today.[65]

This is just one of many ways in which the agendas of the present distort our understanding of the past, forfeiting valuable lessons that a knowledge of the past could teach. At a minimum, the history of slavery should be a grim warning for all time against giving any human beings unbridled power over other human beings, regardless of how attractively that unbridled power might be packaged rhetorically today.

"In history a great volume is unrolled for our instruction, drawing the materials of future wisdom from past errors and infirmities of mankind," as Edmund Burke said, more than two centuries ago. But he warned that the past could also be a means of "keeping alive, or reviving, dissensions and animosities."[66]

The past must be understood in its own context. It cannot be seen as if its context were just like the context of the present, but with events simply taking place in an earlier time. That would be as great an error as failing to understand the implications of the fact that the past is irrevocable. Because human beings can make choices only among options actually available, events in the past can be understood and judged only within the inherent constraints of their particular times and places.

Obvious as all this may seem, it is often forgotten. Nothing that Germans can do today will in any way mitigate the staggering evils of what Hitler did in the past. Nor can apologies in America today for slavery in the past have any meaning, much less do any good, for either blacks or whites today. What can it mean for *A* to apologize for what *B* did, even among contemporaries, much less across the vast chasm between the living and the dead?

The only times over which we have any degree of influence at all are the present and the future— both of which can be made worse by attempts at symbolic restitution among the living for what happened among the dead, who are far beyond our power to help or punish or avenge. Galling as these restrictive facts may be, that does not stop them from being facts beyond our control. Pretending to have powers that we do not, in fact, have risks creating needless evils in the present while claiming to deal with the evils of the past.

Any serious consideration of the world as it is around us today must tell us that maintaining common decency, much less peace and harmony, among living contemporaries is a major challenge, both among nations and within nations. To admit that we can do nothing about what happened among the dead is not to give up the struggle for a better world, but to concentrate our efforts where they have at least some hope of making things better for the living.

ACKNOWLEDGEMENTS

Even a small book such as this, but one dealing with a vast subject, incurs innumerable debts to the works of others, too numerous to name. In addition to the many writings cited in the footnotes and endnotes, there have been many other writings and other sources of insights that provided a background of historical, geographic and economic knowledge, gleaned over the years, without which there would have been no basis for the particular research and analysis that enabled me to "cross-examine the facts," as the great economist Alfred Marshall defined the goal of economic analysis.

Closer to home, commentaries and critiques by my wife Mary, and by my colleagues and friends Joseph Charney and Stephen Camarata, have been very helpful, and the whole enterprise would have been all but impossible, especially at my advanced age, without the dedicated work of my assistants of many years, Na Liu and Elizabeth Costa. The institutional support of the Hoover Institution and the Stanford University libraries has also been indispensable.

In the end, however, none of these can be held responsible for my conclusions, or for any errors or shortcomings that may appear. For all these I must take sole responsibility.

Thomas Sowell
The Hoover Institution
Stanford University

NOTES

Chapter 1: Disparities and Prerequisites

1. *World Illiteracy At Mid-Century: A Statistical Study* (Paris: United Nations Educational, Scientific and Cultural Organization, 1957), p. 15.

2. Malcolm Gladwell, *Outliers: The Story of Success* (New York: Little, Brown and Company, 2008), p. 111.

3. Ibid., pp. 89–90.

4. Ibid., pp. 111–112.

5. Ibid., pp. 111–113.

6. Charles Murray, *Human Accomplishment: The Pursuit of Excellence in the Arts and Sciences, 800 B.C. to 1950* (New York: HarperCollins, 2003), pp. 98–99.

7. Ibid., p. 99.

8. James Corrigan, "Woods in the Mood to End His Major Drought," *The Daily Telegraph* (London), August 5, 2013, pp. 16–17.

9. Charles Murray, *Human Accomplishment*, p. 102.

10. Ibid., pp. 355–361.

11. John K. Fairbank and Edwin O. Reischauer, *China: Tradition & Transformation* (Boston: Houghton Mifflin, 1978), p. 17.

12. William D. Altus, "Birth Order and Its Sequelae," *Science*, Vol. 151 (January 7, 1966), p. 45.

13. Ibid.

14. Julia M. Rohrer, Boris Egloff, and Stefan C. Schmukle, "Examining the Effects of Birth Order on Personality," *Proceedings of the National Academy of Sciences*, Vol. 112, No. 46 (November 17, 2015), p. 14225. These differences in median IQs are not necessarily large. However, even modest differences in median IQs can translate into large disparities in the representation of different groups at IQs of 120 and above— which are the kinds of IQs found among people in elite occupations that attract major attention. Most observers are far less interested in what kinds of people qualify to work behind the counter of fast-food restaurants than they are in what kinds of people are qualified to work in chemistry labs or as engineers or physicians.

15. Lillian Belmont and Francis A. Marolla, "Birth Order, Family Size, and Intelligence," *Science*, Vol. 182 (December 14, 1973), p. 1098.

16. Sandra E. Black, Paul J. Devereux and Kjell G. Salvanes, "Older and Wiser? Birth Order and IQ of Young Men," *CESifo Economic Studies*, Vol. 57, 1/2011, pp. 103–120.

17. Lillian Belmont and Francis A. Marolla, "Birth Order, Family Size, and Intelligence," *Science*, Vol. 182 (December 14, 1973), pp. 1096–1097; Sandra E. Black, Paul J. Devereux and Kjell G. Salvanes, "Older and Wiser? Birth Order and IQ of Young Men," *CESifo Economic Studies*, Vol. 57, 1/2011, p. 109.

18. Sidney Cobb and John R.P. French, Jr., "Birth Order Among Medical Students," *Journal of the American Medical Association*, Vol. 195, No. 4 (January 24, 1966), pp. 172–173.

19. William A Layman and Andrew Saueracker, "Birth Order and Sibship Size of Medical School Applicants," *Social Psychiatry*, Vol. 13 (1978), pp. 117–123.

20. Alison L. Booth and Hiau Joo Kee, "Birth Order Matters: The Effect of Family Size and Birth Order on Educational Attainment," *Journal of Population Economics*, Vol. 22, No. 2 (April 2009), p. 377.

21. Robert J. Gary-Bobo, Ana Prieto and Natalie Picard, "Birth Order and Sibship Sex Composition as Instruments in the Study of Education and Earnings," Discussion Paper No. 5514 (February 2006), Centre for Economic Policy Research, London, p. 22.

22. Jere R. Behrman and Paul Taubman, "Birth Order, Schooling, and Earnings," *Journal of Labor Economics*, Vol. 4, No. 3 Part 2: The Family and the Distribution of Economic Rewards (July 1986), p. S136.

23. Philip S. Very and Richard W. Prull, "Birth Order, Personality Development, and the Choice of Law as a Profession," *Journal of Genetic Psychology*, Vol. 116, No. 2 (June 1, 1970), pp. 219–221.

24. Richard L. Zweigenhaft, "Birth Order, Approval-Seeking and Membership in Congress," *Journal of Individual Psychology*, Vol. 31, No. 2 (November 1975), p. 208.

25. *Astronauts and Cosmonauts: Biographical and Statistical Data*, Revised August 31, 1993, Report Prepared by the Congressional Research Service, Library of Congress, Transmitted to the Committee on Science, Space, and Technology, U.S. House of Representatives, One Hundred Third Congress, Second Session, March 1994 (Washington: U.S. Government Printing Office, 1994), p. 19.

26. Daniel S.P. Schubert, Mazie E. Wagner, and Herman J.P. Schubert, "Family Constellation and Creativity: Firstborn Predominance Among Classical Music Composers," *The Journal of Psychology*, Vol. 95, No. 1 (1977), pp. 147–149.

27. Arthur R. Jensen, *Genetics and Education* (New York: Harper & Row, 1972), p. 143.

28. R.G. Record, Thomas McKeown and J.H. Edwards, "An Investigation of the Difference in Measured Intelligence Between Twins and Single Births," *Annals of Human Genetics*, Vol. 34, Issue 1 (July 1970), pp. 18, 19, 20.

29. "Choose Your Parents Wisely," *The Economist*, July 26, 2014, p. 22.

30. Edward C. Banfield, *The Unheavenly City* (Boston: Little, Brown, 1970), pp. 224–229.

31. For examples and a fuller discussion of social mobility see Thomas Sowell, *Wealth, Poverty and Politics*, revised and enlarged edition (New York: Basic Books, 2016), pp. 178–183, 369–375.

32. Henry Thomas Buckle, *On Scotland and the Scotch Intellect* (Chicago: University of Chicago Press, 1970), p. 52.

33. Irokawa Daikichi, *The Culture of the Meiji Period*, translated and edited by Marius B. Jansen (Princeton: Princeton University Press, 1985), p. 7.

34. Joel Mokyr, *A Culture of Growth: The Origins of the Modern Economy* (Princeton: Princeton University Press, 2017), p. 256.

35. Steven Beller, "Big-City Jews: Jewish Big City— the Dialectics of Jewish Assimilation in Vienna, *c.* 1900," *The City in Central Europe: Culture and Society from 1800 to the Present*, edited by Malcolm Gee, Tim Kirk and Jill Steward (Brookfield, Vermont: Ashgate Publishing, Ltd., 1999), p. 150.

36. Charles Murray, *Human Accomplishment*, pp. 280, 282.

37. Charles O. Hucker, *China's Imperial Past: An Introduction to Chinese History and Culture* (Stanford: Stanford University Press, 1975), p. 65; Jacques Gernet, *A History of Chinese Civilization*, second edition, translated by J.R. Foster and Charles Hartman (New York: Cambridge University Press, 1996), p. 69.

38. David S. Landes, *The Wealth and Poverty of Nations: Why Some Are So Rich and Some So Poor* (New York: W.W. Norton & Company, 1998), pp. 93–95; William H. McNeill, *The Rise of the West: A History of the Human Community* (Chicago: University of Chicago Press, 1991), p. 526.

39. David S. Landes, *The Wealth and Poverty of Nations*, pp. 94–95.

40. See, for examples, Thomas Sowell, *Wealth, Poverty and Politics*, revised and enlarged edition, especially Part I; Ellen Churchill Semple, *Influences of Geographic Environment* (New York: Henry Holt and Company, 1911), pp. 144, 175, 397, 530, 531, 599, 600. By contrast, she refers to "the cosmopolitan civilization characteristic of coastal regions." Ibid., p. 347.

41. Andrew Tanzer, "The Bamboo Network," *Forbes*, July 18, 1994, pp. 138–144; "China: Seeds of Subversion," *The Economist*, May 28, 1994, p. 32.

42. Richard Rhodes, *The Making of the Atomic Bomb* (New York: Simon & Schuster, 1986), pp. 13, 106, 188–189, 305–314; Silvan S. Schweber, *Einstein and Oppenheimer: The Meaning of Genius* (Cambridge, Massachusetts: Harvard University Press, 2008), p. 138; Michio Kaku, *Einstein's Cosmos: How Albert Einstein's Vision Transformed Our Understanding of Space and Time* (New York: W.W. Norton, 2004), pp. 187–188; Howard M. Sachar, *A History of the Jews in America* (New York: Alfred A. Knopf, 1992), p. 527; American Jewish Historical Society, *American Jewish Desk Reference* (New York: Random House, 1999), p. 591.

43. Quoted in Bernard Lewis, *The Muslim Discovery of Europe* (New York: W.W. Norton, 1982), p. 139.

44. Giovanni Gavetti, Rebecca Henderson and Simona Giorgi, "Kodak and the Digital Revolution (A)," 9–705–448, Harvard Business School, November 2, 2005, pp. 3, 11.

45. "The Last Kodak Moment?" *The Economist*, January 14, 2012, pp. 63–64.

46. Mike Spector and Dana Mattioli, "Can Bankruptcy Filing Save Kodak?" *Wall Street Journal*, January 20, 2012, p. B1.

47. Henry C. Lucas, Jr., *Inside the Future: Surviving the Technology Revolution* (Westport, Connecticut: Praeger, 2008), p. 157.

48. Giovanni Gavetti, Rebecca Henderson and Simona Giorgi, "Kodak and the Digital Revolution (A)," 9–705–448, Harvard Business School, November 2, 2005, p. 4.

49. Ibid., p. 12.

50. Karen Kaplan, "Man, Chimp Separated by a Dab of DNA," *Los Angeles Times*, September 1, 2005, p. A12; Rick Weiss, "Scientists Complete Genetic Map of the Chimpanzee," *Washington Post*, September 1, 2005, p. A3; "A Creeping Success," *The Economist*, June 5, 1999, pp. 77–78.

51. Darrell Hess, *McKnight's Physical Geography: A Landscape Appreciation*, eleventh edition (Upper Saddle River, New Jersey: Pearson Education, Inc., 2014), p. 200.

52. *Africa: Atlas of Our Changing Environment* (Nairobi, Kenya: United Nations Environment Programme, 2008), p. 29; Rachel I. Albrecht, Steven J. Goodman, Dennis E. Buechler, Richard J. Blakeslee and Hugh J. Christian, "Where Are the Lightning Hotspots on Earth?" *Bulletin of the American Meteorological Society*, November 2016, p. 2055; *The New Encyclopædia Britannica* (Chicago: Encyclopædia Britannica, Inc., 2005), Volume 3, p. 583.

53. Alan H. Strahler, *Introducing Physical Geography*, sixth edition (Hoboken, New Jersey: Wiley, 2013), pp. 402–403.

54. Bradley C. Bennett, "Plants and People of the Amazonian Rainforests," *BioScience*, Vol. 42, No. 8 (September 1992), p. 599.

55. Ronald Fraser, "The Amazon," *Great Rivers of the World*, edited by Alexander Frater (Boston: Little, Brown and Company, 1984), p. 111.

56. David S. Landes, *The Wealth and Poverty of Nations*, p. 6.

57. See, for example, Ellen Churchill Semple, *Influences of Geographic Environment*, pp. 20, 280, 281–282, 347, 521–531, 599, 600; Fernand Braudel, *The Mediterranean and the Mediterranean World in the Age of Philip II*, translated by Siân Reynolds (Berkeley: University of California Press, 1995), Vol. I, pp. 34, 35; Thomas Sowell, *Wealth, Poverty and Politics*, revised and enlarged edition, pp. 45–54.

58. See, for example, Frederick R. Troeh and Louis M. Thompson, *Soils and Soil Fertility*, sixth edition (Ames, Iowa: Blackwell, 2005), p. 330; Xiaobing Liu, et al., "Overview of Mollisols in the World: Distribution, Land Use and Management," *Canadian Journal of Soil Science*, Vol. 92 (2012), pp. 383–402; Darrel Hess, *McKnight's Physical Geography*, eleventh edition, pp. 362–363.

59. Andrew D. Mellinger, Jeffrey D. Sachs, and John L. Gallup, "Climate, Coastal Proximity, and Development," *The Oxford Handbook of Economic Geography*, edited by Gordon L. Clark, Maryann P. Feldman and Meric S. Gertler (Oxford: Oxford University Press, 2000), p. 169.

Chapter 2: Discrimination: Meanings and Costs

1.   Harry J. Holzer, Steven Raphael, and Michael A. Stoll, "Perceived Criminality, Criminal Background Checks, and the Racial Hiring Practices of Employers," *Journal of Law and Economics*, Vol. 49, No. 2 (October 2006), pp. 452, 473.

2.   Jason L. Riley, "Jobless Blacks Should Cheer Background Checks," *Wall Street Journal*, August 23, 2013, p. A11; Paul Sperry, "Background Checks Are Racist?" *Investor's Business Daily*, March 28, 2014, p. A1.

3.   See, for example, Zy Weinberg, "No Place to Shop: Food Access Lacking in the Inner City," *Race, Poverty & the Environment*, Vol. 7, No. 2 (Winter 2000), pp. 22–24; Michael E. Porter, "The Competitive Advantage of the Inner City," *Harvard Business Review*, May-June 1995, pp. 63–64; James M. MacDonald and Paul E. Nelson, Jr., "Do the Poor Still Pay More? Food Price Variations in Large Metropolitan Areas," *Journal of Urban Economics*, Vol. 30 (1991), pp. 349, 350, 357; Donald R. Marion, "Toward Revitalizing Inner-City Food Retailing," *National Food Review*, Summer 1982, pp. 22, 23, 24.

4.   David Caplovitz, *The Poor Pay More: Consumer Practices of Low-Income Families* (New York: The Free Press, 1967), p. xvi.

5.   See, for example, "Democrats Score A.&P. Over Prices," *New York Times*, July 18, 1963, p. 11; Elizabeth Shelton, "Prices Are Never Right," *Washington Post*, December 4, 1964, p. C3; "Gouging the Poor," *New York Times*, August 13, 1966, p. 41; "Overpricing of Food in Slums Is Alleged at House Hearing," *New York Times*, October 13, 1967, p. 20; "Ghetto Cheats Blamed for Urban Riots," *Chicago Tribune*, February 18, 1968, p. 8; "Business Leaders Urge Actions to Help Poor," *Los Angeles Times*, April 11, 1968, p. C13; Frederick D. Sturdivant and Walter T. Wilhelm, "Poverty, Minorities, and Consumer Exploitation," *Social Science Quarterly*, Vol. 49, No. 3 (December 1968), p. 650.

6.   Donald R. Marion, "Toward Revitalizing Inner-City Food Retailing," *National Food Review*, Summer 1982, pp. 23–24. "Sales in urban stores are 13 percent lower by volume, and operating costs are 9 percent higher. Profits, before taxes, are less than half of the suburban stores. Labor costs are higher, shrinkage costs are greater, sales per customer are lower, insurance and repair costs are higher, and losses due to crime are more than doubled in the inner-city stores." *Hearings Before the Subcommittee on Agricultural Production, Marketing, and Stabilization of Prices of the Committee on Agriculture and*

Forestry, United States Senate, Ninety-Fourth Congress, Second Session, June 23 and 25, 1976 (Washington: U.S. Government Printing Office, 1976), p. 57. See also pp. 116, 124–125.

7. "They view Blacks as their personal preserve, their field of plunder where extraordinary profits have and can be made at the expense of our community." "The Poor Pay More…for Less," *New York Amsterdam News*, April 20, 1991, p. 12.

8. Dorothy Height, "A Woman's Word," *New York Amsterdam News*, July 24, 1965, p. 34.

9. Ray Cooklis, "Lowering the High Cost of Being Poor," *Cincinnati Enquirer*, May 28, 2009, p. A7.

10. Jonathan Gill, *Harlem: The Four Hundred Year History from Dutch Village to Capital of Black America* (New York: Grove Press, 2011), p. 119.

11. See U.S. Census Bureau, B01002, Median Age by Sex, Universe: Total Population, 2011–2015 American Community Survey Selected Population Tables.

12. "Choose Your Parents Wisely," *The Economist*, July 26, 2014, p. 22.

13. *The Chronicle of Higher Education: Almanac 2014–2015*, August 22, 2014, p. 4.

14. Karl Marx and Frederick Engels, *Selected Correspondence 1846–1895*, translated by Dona Torr (New York: International Publishers, 1942), p. 476.

15. Adam Smith, *The Wealth of Nations* (New York: Modern Library, 1937), p. 423.

16. Adam Smith denounced "the mean rapacity, the monopolizing spirit of merchants and manufacturers" and "the clamour and sophistry of merchants and manufacturers," whom he characterized as people who "seldom meet together, even for merriment and diversion, but the conversation ends in a conspiracy against the public." As for policies recommended by such people, Smith said: "The proposal of any new law or regulation of commerce which comes from this order, ought always to be listened to with great precaution, and ought never to be adopted till after having been long and carefully examined, not only with the most scrupulous, but with the most suspicious attention. It comes from an order of men, whose interest is never exactly the same with that of the public, who have generally an interest to deceive and even to oppress the public, and who accordingly have, upon many occasions, both deceived and oppressed it." Adam Smith, *The Wealth of Nations*, pp. 128, 250, 460. Karl Marx

wrote, in the preface to the first volume of *Capital*: "I paint the capitalist and the landlord in no sense *couleur de rose*. But here individuals are dealt with only in so far as they are the personifications of economic categories, embodiments of particular class-relations and class-interests. My stand-point, from which the evolution of the economic formation of society is viewed as a process of natural history, can less than any other make the individual responsible for relations whose creature he socially remains, however much he may subjectively raise himself above them." In Chapter X, Marx made dire predictions about the fate of workers, but not as a result of subjective moral deficiencies of the capitalist, for Marx said: "As capitalist, he is only capital personified" and "all this does not, indeed, depend on the good or ill will of the individual capitalist." Karl Marx, *Capital: A Critique of Political Economy* (Chicago: Charles H. Kerr & Company, 1909), Vol. I, pp. 15, 257, 297.

17. William Julius Wilson, *The Declining Significance of Race: Blacks and Changing American Institutions*, third edition (Chicago: University of Chicago Press, 2012), pp. 52–53, 54–55, 59.

18. Robert Higgs, *Competition and Coercion: Blacks in the American Economy 1865–1914* (New York: Cambridge University Press, 1977), pp. 47–49, 130–131.

19. Ibid., pp. 102, 144–146.

20. Ibid., p. 117.

21. Walter E. Williams, *South Africa's War Against Capitalism* (New York: Praeger, 1989), pp. 101, 102, 103, 104, 105.

22. The book that resulted from this research was Walter E. Williams, *South Africa's War Against Capitalism*.

23. Ibid., pp. 112, 113.

24. See, for example, Thomas Sowell, *Applied Economics: Thinking Beyond Stage One*, revised and enlarged edition (New York: Basic Books, 2009), Chapter 7; Thomas Sowell, *Economic Facts and Fallacies* (New York: Basic Books, 2008), pp. 73–75, 123, 170–172.

25. Jennifer Roback, "The Political Economy of Segregation: The Case of Segregated Streetcars," *Journal of Economic History*, Vol. 46, No. 4 (December 1986), pp. 893–917.

26. Ibid., pp. 894, 899–901, 903, 904, 912, 916.

27. Kermit L. Hall and John J. Patrick, *The Pursuit of Justice: Supreme Court Decisions that Shaped America* (New York: Oxford University Press, 2006), pp. 59–64; Michael J. Klarman, *From Jim Crow to Civil Rights: The Supreme Court and the Struggle for Racial Equality* (Oxford: Oxford University Press, 2004), p. 8.

28. Bernard E. Anderson, *Negro Employment in Public Utilities: A Study of Racial Policies in the Electric Power, Gas, and Telephone Industries* (Philadelphia: University of Pennsylvania Press, 1970), pp. 73, 80.

29. Ibid., pp. 93–95.

30. Venus Green, *Race on the Line: Gender, Labor, and Technology in the Bell System, 1880–1980* (Durham: Duke University Press, 2001), p. 210.

31. Bernard E. Anderson, *Negro Employment in Public Utilities*, pp. 150, 152. During the 1950s, the percentage of male employees in the telecommunications industry who were black actually fell in such Southern states as Alabama, Arkansas, Florida, Georgia, Kentucky, Louisiana, Mississippi, North Carolina, South Carolina, Tennessee, Texas and Virginia. Ibid., pp. 84–87.

32. Ibid., pp. 84–87.

33. Ibid., pp. 114, 139.

34. Michael R. Winston, "Through the Back Door: Academic Racism and the Negro Scholar in Historical Perspective," *Daedalus*, Vol. 100, No. 3 (Summer 1971), pp. 695, 705.

35. Milton & Rose D. Friedman, *Two Lucky People: Memoirs* (Chicago: University of Chicago Press, 1998), pp. 91–92, 94–95, 105–106, 153–154.

36. Greg Robinson, "Davis, Allison," *Encyclopedia of African-American Culture and History*, edited by Colin A. Palmer (Detroit: Thomson-Gale, 2006), Volume C–F, p. 583; "The Talented Black Scholars Whom No White University Would Hire," *Journal of Blacks in Higher Education*, No. 58 (Winter 2007/2008), p. 81.

37. George J. Stigler, "The Economics of Minimum Wage Legislation," *American Economic Review*, Vol. 36, No. 3 (June 1946), p. 358.

38. Walter E. Williams, *Race & Economics: How Much Can Be Blamed on Discrimination* (Stanford: Hoover Institution Press, 2011), pp. 42–43.

39. Ibid.; Edward C. Banfield, *The Unheavenly City* (Boston: Little, Brown, 1970), p. 98.

40. Charles Murray, *Losing Ground: American Social Policy, 1950–1980* (New York: Basic Books, 1984), p. 77.

41. Jason B. Johnson, "Making Ends Meet: Struggling in Middle Class," *San Francisco Chronicle*, October 16, 2005, p. A11.

42. Stephen Coyle, "Palo Alto: A Far Cry from *Euclid*," *Land Use and Housing on the San Francisco Peninsula*, edited by Thomas M. Hagler (Stanford: Stanford Environmental Law Society, 1983), pp. 85, 89.

43. Hans P. Johnson and Amanda Bailey, "California's Newest Homeowners: Affording the Unaffordable," *California Counts: Population Trends and Profiles* (Public Policy Institute of California), Vol. 7, No. 1 (August 2005), p. 4.

44. Leslie Fulbright, "S.F. Moves to Stem African American Exodus," *San Francisco Chronicle*, April 9, 2007, p. A1.

45. Bureau of the Census, *1990 Census of Population: General Population Characteristics California*, 1990 CP–1–6, Section 1 of 3, pp. 27, 28, 31; U.S. Census Bureau, *Profiles of General Demographic Characteristics 2000: 2000 Census of Population and Housing, California*, Table DP–1, pp. 2, 20, 42.

46. Gilbert Osofsky, *Harlem: The Making of a Ghetto, Negro New York 1890–1930* (New York: Harper & Row, 1966), pp. 106–110; Jonathan Gill, *Harlem*, pp. 180–184.

47. Gilbert Osofsky, *Harlem*, p. 110.

Chapter 3: Sorting and Unsorting People

1. Joses C. Moya, *Cousins and Strangers: Spanish Immigrants in Buenos Aires, 1850–1930* (Berkeley: University of California Press, 1998), pp. 119, 145–146.

2. Jonathan Gill, *Harlem: The Four Hundred Year History from Dutch Village to Capital of Black America* (New York: Grove Press, 2011), p. 140; Charles A. Price, *Southern Europeans in Australia* (Melbourne: Oxford University Press, 1963), p. 162; Philip Taylor, *The Distant Magnet: European Emigration to the USA* (New York: Harper & Row, 1971), pp. 210, 211; Dino Cinel, *From Italy to San Francisco: The Immigrant Experience* (Stanford: Stanford University Press, 1982), pp. 28, 117–120; Samuel L. Baily, "The Adjustment of Italian

Immigrants in Buenos Aires and New York, 1870–1914," *American Historical Review*, April 1983, p. 291; John E. Zucchi, *Italians in Toronto: Development of a National Identity, 1875–1935* (Kingston, Ontario: McGill-Queen's University Press, 1988), pp. 41, 53–55, 58.

3. Annie Polland and Daniel Soyer, *Emerging Metropolis: New York Jews in the Age of Immigration, 1840–1920* (New York: New York University Press, 2012), p. 31; Tyler Anbinder, *City of Dreams: The 400-Year Epic History of Immigrant New York* (Boston: Houghton Mifflin Harcourt, 2016), pp. 174–175, 178, 356, 358; Moses Rischin, *The Promised City: New York's Jews 1870–1914* (Cambridge, Massachusetts: Harvard University Press, 1962), pp. 76, 85–108, 238–239; Stephen Birmingham, *"The Rest of Us": The Rise of America's Eastern European Jews* (Boston: Little, Brown, 1984), pp. 12–24.

4. Louis Wirth, *The Ghetto* (Chicago: University of Chicago Press, 1956), pp. 182–184; Irving Cutler, "The Jews of Chicago: From Shetl to Suburb," *Ethnic Chicago: A Multicultural Portrait*, fourth edition, edited by Melvin G. Holli and Peter d'A. Jones (Grand Rapids, Michigan: William B. Eerdmans Publishing Company, 1995), pp. 127–129, 134–135, 143–144.

5. H.L. van der Laan, *The Lebanese Traders in Sierra Leone* (The Hague: Mouton & Co., 1975), pp. 237–240; Louise L'Estrange Fawcett, "Lebanese, Palestinians and Syrians in Colombia," *The Lebanese in the World: A Century of Emigration*, edited by Albert Hourani and Nadim Shehadi (London: The Centre for Lebanese Studies, 1992), p. 368.

6. Tyler Anbinder, *City of Dreams*, pp. 176–177.

7. Teiiti Suzuki, *The Japanese Immigrant in Brazil: Narrative Part* (Tokyo: University of Tokyo Press, 1969), p. 109.

8. Tyler Anbinder, *City of Dreams*, p. 185.

9. Charles A. Price, *The Methods and Statistics of 'Southern Europeans in Australia'* (Canberra: The Australian National University, 1963), p. 45.

10. E. Franklin Frazier, "The Negro Family in Chicago," *E. Franklin Frazier on Race Relations: Selected Writings*, edited by G. Franklin Edwards (Chicago: University of Chicago Press, 1968), pp. 122–126.

11. E. Franklin Frazier, "The Impact of Urban Civilization Upon Negro Family Life," *American Sociological Review*, Vol. 2, No. 5 (October 1937), p. 615.

12. David M. Katzman, *Before the Ghetto: Black Detroit in the Nineteenth Century* (Urbana: University of Illinois Press, 1973), p. 27.

13. Kenneth L. Kusmer, *A Ghetto Takes Shape: Black Cleveland, 1870–1930* (Urbana: University of Illinois Press, 1978), p. 209.

14. Jonathan Gill, *Harlem*, p. 284.

15. Andrew F. Brimmer, "The Labor Market and the Distribution of Income," *Reflections of America: Commemorating the Statistical Abstract Centennial*, edited by Norman Cousins (Washington: U.S. Department of Commerce, Bureau of the Census, 1980), pp. 102–103.

16. William Julius Wilson, *When Work Disappears: The World of the New Urban Poor* (New York: Alfred A. Knopf, 1996), p. 195.

17. Horace Mann Bond, *A Study of Factors Involved in the Identification and Encouragement of Unusual Academic Talent among Underprivileged Populations* (U.S. Department of Health, Education, and Welfare, January 1967), p. 147. [Contract No. SAE 8028, Project No. 5–0859].

18. Ibid.

19. See, for example, Willard B. Gatewood, *Aristocrats of Color: The Black Elite, 1880–1920* (Bloomington: Indiana University Press, 1990), pp. 188–189, 247; David M. Katzman, *Before the Ghetto*, Chapter V; Theodore Hershberg and Henry Williams, "Mulattoes and Blacks: Intra-Group Differences and Social Stratification in Nineteenth-Century Philadelphia," *Philadelphia: Work, Space, Family, and Group Experience in the Nineteenth Century*, edited by Theodore Hershberg (Oxford: Oxford University Press, 1981), pp. 392–434.

20. Stephen Birmingham, *Certain People: America's Black Elite* (Boston: Little, Brown and Company, 1977), pp. 196–197. As a personal note, I delivered groceries to people in that building during my teenage years, entering through the service entrance in the basement, rather than through the canopied front entrance with its uniformed doorman and ornate lobby. My own home was in a tenement apartment some distance away.

21. St. Clair Drake and Horace R. Cayton, *Black Metropolis: A Study of Negro Life in a Northern City*, revised and enlarged edition (Chicago: University of Chicago Press, 1993), pp. 73–74; James R. Grossman, "African-American Migration to Chicago," *Ethnic Chicago*, fourth edition, edited by Melvin G. Holli and Peter d'A. Jones, pp. 323, 332, 333–334; Henri Florette, *Black*

Migration: Movement North, 1900–1920 (Garden City, New York: Anchor Press, 1975), pp. 96–97; Allan H. Spear, *Black Chicago: The Making of a Negro Ghetto, 1890–1920* (Chicago: University of Chicago Press, 1967), p. 168.

22. James R. Grossman, "African-American Migration to Chicago," *Ethnic Chicago*, fourth edition, edited by Melvin G. Holli and Peter d'A. Jones, pp. 323, 330, 332, 333–334; Willard B. Gatewood, *Aristocrats of Color*, pp. 186–187, 332; Allan H. Spear, *Black Chicago*, p. 168; E. Franklin Frazier, *The Negro in the United States*, revised edition (New York: Macmillan, 1957), p. 284; Henri Florette, *Black Migration*, pp. 96–97; Gilbert Osofsky, *Harlem: The Making of a Ghetto, Negro New York 1890–1930* (New York: Harper & Row, 1966), pp. 43–44; Ivan H. Light, *Ethnic Enterprise in America: Business and Welfare Among Chinese, Japanese, and Blacks* (Berkeley: University of California Press, 1972), Figure 1 (after p. 100); W.E.B. Du Bois, *The Black North in 1901: A Social Study* (New York: Arno Press, 1969), p. 25.

23. James R. Grossman, "African-American Migration to Chicago," *Ethnic Chicago*, fourth edition, edited by Melvin G. Holli and Peter d'A. Jones, p. 331; See also Ethan Michaeli, *The Defender: How the Legendary Black Newspaper Changed America* (Boston: Houghton Mifflin Harcourt, 2016), p. 84.

24. Willard B. Gatewood, *Aristocrats of Color*, pp. 186–187; James R. Grossman, "African-American Migration to Chicago," *Ethnic Chicago*, fourth edition, edited by Melvin G. Holli and Peter d'A. Jones, pp. 323, 330; St. Clair Drake and Horace R. Cayton, *Black Metropolis*, revised and enlarged edition, pp. 73–74.

25. E. Franklin Frazier, *The Negro in the United States*, revised edition, p. 643.

26. According to Professor Steven Pinker, "the North-South difference is not a by-product of the white-black difference. Southern whites are more violent than northern whites, and southern blacks are more violent than northern blacks." Steven Pinker, *The Better Angels of Our Nature: Why Violence Has Declined* (New York: Viking, 2011), p. 94.

27. Davison M. Douglas, *Jim Crow Moves North: The Battle over Northern School Segregation, 1865–1954* (Cambridge: Cambridge University Press, 2005), pp. 2–5, 61–62; Willard B. Gatewood, *Aristocrats of Color*, p. 250; E. Franklin Frazier, *The Negro in the United States*, revised edition, p. 441.

28. Willard B. Gatewood, *Aristocrats of Color*, pp. 64, 65, 300–301; E. Franklin Frazier, *The Negro in the United States*, revised edition, pp. 250–251.

29. Davison M. Douglas, *Jim Crow Moves North*, pp. 128, 129; Kenneth L. Kusmer, *A Ghetto Takes Shape*, pp. 57, 64–65, 75–76, 80, 178–179.

30. Davison M. Douglas, *Jim Crow Moves North*, pp. 130–131; Willard B. Gatewood, *Aristocrats of Color*, p. 147.

31. Marilynn S. Johnson, *The Second Gold Rush: Oakland and the East Bay in World War II* (Berkeley: University of California Press, 1993), p. 198.

32. Douglas Henry Daniels, *Pioneer Urbanites: A Social and Cultural History of Black San Francisco* (Philadelphia: Temple University Press, 1980), pp. 50, 75, 77, 97.

33. Marilynn S. Johnson, *The Second Gold Rush*, p. 52.

34. Ibid., p. 55.

35. Douglas Henry Daniels, *Pioneer Urbanites*, p. 165.

36. Marilynn S. Johnson, *The Second Gold Rush*, pp. 95–96, 152, 170; E. Franklin Frazier, *The Negro in the United States*, revised edition, p. 270; Douglas Henry Daniels, *Pioneer Urbanites*, pp. 171–175.

37. E. Franklin Frazier, *The Negro in the United States*, revised edition, p. 270.

38. Arthur R. Jensen, *Genetics and Education* (New York: Harper & Row, 1972), pp. 106–107, 129–130.

39. William Julius Wilson, *More Than Just Race: Being Black and Poor in the Inner City* (New York: W.W. Norton & Company, 2009), pp. 1–2.

40. Walter E. Williams, *Race & Economics: How Much Can Be Blamed on Discrimination* (Stanford: Hoover Institution Press, 2011), p. 117.

41. See Abbot Emerson Smith, *Colonists in Bondage: White Servitude and Convict Labor in America 1607–1776* (Gloucester, Massachusetts: Peter Smith, 1965), pp. 3–4.

42. E. Franklin Frazier, *The Negro in the United States*, revised edition, pp. 22–26; John Hope Franklin, *From Slavery to Freedom: A History of American Negroes*, second edition (New York: Alfred A. Knopf, 1947), pp. 70–72.

43. Steven Pinker, *The Better Angels of Our Nature*, p. 97.

44. St. Clair Drake and Horace R. Cayton, *Black Metropolis*, revised and enlarged edition, pp. 44–45.

45. David M. Katzman, *Before the Ghetto*, pp. 35, 69, 102, 200.

46. Ibid., p. 160.

47. W.E.B. Du Bois, *The Philadelphia Negro: A Social Study* (New York: Schocken Books, 1967), pp. 7, 41–42, 305–306.

48. Jacob Riis, *How the Other Half Lives: Studies among the Tenements of New York* (Cambridge, Massachusetts: Harvard University Press, 1970), p. 99; David M. Katzman, *Before the Ghetto*, pp. 35, 37, 138, 139, 160; St. Clair Drake and Horace R. Cayton, *Black Metropolis*, revised and enlarged edition, pp. 44–45; Willard B. Gatewood, *Aristocrats of Color*, p. 125.

49. Davison M. Douglas, *Jim Crow Moves North*, p. 3.

50. Jacob Riis, *How the Other Half Lives*, p. 99.

51. Davison M. Douglas, *Jim Crow Moves North*, p. 3.

52. Ibid., pp. 155–156.

53. Ibid., pp. 154.

54. See, for example, Jacqueline A. Stefkovich and Terrence Leas, "A Legal History of Desegregation in Higher Education," *Journal of Negro Education*, Vol. 63, No. 3 (Summer 1994), pp. 409–410.

55. *Brown v. Board of Education of Topeka*, 347 U.S. 483 (1954), at 495.

56. Ibid., at 494.

57. T. Rees Shapiro, "Vanished Glory of an All-Black High School," *Washington Post*, January 19, 2014, p. B6.

58. Henry S. Robinson, "The M Street High School, 1891–1916," *Records of the Columbia Historical Society*, Washington, D.C., Vol. LI (1984), p. 122; *Report of the Board of Trustees of Public Schools of the District of Columbia to the Commissioners of the District of Columbia: 1898–99* (Washington: Government Printing Office, 1900), pp. 7, 11.

59. Mary Gibson Hundley, *The Dunbar Story: 1870–1955* (New York: Vantage Press, 1965), p. 75.

60. Ibid., p. 78. Mary Church Terrell, "History of the High School for Negroes in Washington," *Journal of Negro History*, Vol. 2, No. 3 (July 1917), p. 262.

61. Louise Daniel Hutchison, *Anna J. Cooper: A Voice from the South* (Washington: The Smithsonian Institution Press, 1981), p. 62; Jervis Anderson, "A Very Special Monument," *The New Yorker*, March 20, 1978, p. 100; Alison Stewart, *First Class: The Legacy of Dunbar, America's First Black Public High School* (Chicago: Lawrence Hill Books, 2013), p. 99; "The Talented Black Scholars

Whom No White University Would Hire," *Journal of Blacks in Higher Education*, No. 58 (Winter 2007/2008), p. 81.

62. Tucker Carlson, "From Ivy League to NBA," *Policy Review*, Spring 1993, p. 36.

63. Daniel Bergner, "Class Warfare," *New York Times Magazine*, September 7, 2014, p. 62.

64. See, for example, Alex Kotlowitz, "Where Is Everyone Going?" *Chicago Tribune*, March 10, 2002; Mary Mitchell, "Middle-Class Neighborhood Fighting to Keep Integrity," *Chicago Sun-Times*, November 10, 2005, p. 14; Jessica Garrison and Ted Rohrlich, "A Not-So-Welcome Mat," *Los Angeles Times*, June 17, 2007, p. A1; Paul Elias, "Influx of Black Renters Raises Tension in Bay Area," *The Associated Press*, December 31, 2008; Mick Dumke, "Unease in Chatham, But Who's at Fault?" *New York Times*, April 29, 2011, p. A23; James Bovard, "Raising Hell in Subsidized Housing," *Wall Street Journal*, August 18, 2011, p. A15; Frank Main, "Crime Felt from CHA Relocations," *Chicago Sun-Times*, April 5, 2012, p. 18.

65. Alex Kotlowitz, "Where Is Everyone Going?" *Chicago Tribune*, March 10, 2002.

66. Mary Mitchell, "Middle-Class Neighborhood Fighting to Keep Integrity," *Chicago Sun-Times*, November 10, 2005, p. 14.

67. Mick Dumke, "Unease in Chatham, But Who's at Fault?" *New York Times*, April 29, 2011, p. A23.

68. Gary Gilbert, "People Must Get Involved in Section 8 Reform," *Contra Costa Times*, November 18, 2006, p. F4.

69. Geetha Suresh and Gennaro F. Vito, "Homicide Patterns and Public Housing: The Case of Louisville, KY (1989–2007), *Homicide Studies*, Vol. 13, No. 4 (November 2009), pp. 411–433.

70. Alex Kotlowitz, "Where Is Everyone Going?" *Chicago Tribune*, March 10, 2002.

71. Ibid.

72. J.D. Vance, *Hillbilly Elegy: A Memoir of a Family and Culture in Crisis* (New York: HarperCollins, 2016), p. 140.

73. Ibid., p. 141.

74. Lisa Sanbonmatsu, Jeffrey R. Kling, Greg J. Duncan and Jeanne Brooks-Gunn, "Neighborhoods and Academic Achievement: Results from the

Moving to Opportunity Experiment," *The Journal of Human Resources*, Vol. 41, No. 4 (Fall, 2006), p. 682.

75. Jens Ludwig, et al., "What Can We Learn about Neighborhood Effects from the Moving to Opportunity Experiment?" *American Journal of Sociology*, Vol. 114, No. 1 (July 2008), p. 148.

76. Jeffrey R. Kling, et al., "Experimental Analysis of Neighborhood Effects," *Econometrica*, Vol. 75, No. 1 (January, 2007), p. 99.

77. Jens Ludwig, et al., "Long-Term Neighborhood Effects on Low-Income Families: Evidence from Moving to Opportunity," *American Economic Review*, Vol. 103, No. 3 (May 2013), p. 227.

78. Lawrence F. Katz, Jeffrey R. Kling, and Jeffrey B. Liebman, "Moving to Opportunity in Boston: Early Results of a Randomized Mobility Experiment," *Quarterly Journal of Economics*, Vol. 116, No. 2 (May 2001), p. 648.

79. *Moving To Opportunity for Fair Housing Demonstration Program: Final Impacts Evaluation, Summary* (Washington: U.S. Department of Housing and Urban Development, November 2011), p. 3.

80. "HUD's Plan to Diversify Suburbs," *Investor's Business Daily*, July 23, 2013, p. A12.

81. Ibid.

82. See, for example, Raj Chetty, Nathaniel Hendren, and Lawrence F. Katz, "The Effects of Exposure to Better Neighborhoods on Children: New Evidence from the Moving to Opportunity Experiment," *American Economic Review*, Vol. 106, No. 4 (April 2016), pp. 857, 899; Lawrence F. Katz, Jeffrey R. Kling, and Jeffrey B. Liebman, "Moving to Opportunity in Boston: Early Results of a Randomized Mobility Experiment," *Quarterly Journal of Economics*, Vol. 116, No. 2 (May 2001), pp. 607, 611–612, 648.

83. *Equal Employment Opportunity Commission v. Sears, Roebuck & Company*, 839 F.2d 302 at 311, 360; Peter Brimelow, "Spiral of Silence," *Forbes*, May 25, 1992, p. 77.

84. Paul Sperry, "Background Checks Are Racist?" *Investor's Business Daily*, March 28, 2014, p. A1.

85. Harry J. Holzer, Steven Raphael, and Michael A. Stoll, "Perceived Criminality, Criminal Background Checks, and the Racial Hiring Practices of Employers," *Journal of Law and Economics*, Vol. 49, No. 2 (October 2006), pp. 451–480.

86. Jason L. Riley, "Jobless Blacks Should Cheer Background Checks," *Wall Street Journal*, August 23, 2013, p. A11; Paul Sperry, "Background Checks Are Racist?" *Investor's Business Daily*, March 28, 2014, p. A1.

87. Douglas P. Woodward, "Locational Determinants of Japanese Manufacturing Start-ups in the United States," *Southern Economic Journal*, Vol. 58, Issue 3 (January 1992), pp. 700, 706; Robert E. Cole and Donald R. Deskins, Jr., "Racial Factors in Site Location and Employment Patterns of Japanese Auto Firms in America," *California Management Review*, Fall 1988, pp. 17–18.

88. Philip S. Foner, "The Rise of the Black Industrial Working Class, 1915–1918," *African Americans in the U.S. Economy*, edited by Cecilia A. Conrad, et al (Lanham, Maryland: Rowman and Littlefield, 2005), pp. 38–43; Leo Alilunas, "Statutory Means of Impeding Emigration of the Negro," *Journal of Negro History*, Vol. 22, No. 2 (April 1937), pp. 148–162; Carole Marks, "Lines of Communication, Recruitment Mechanisms, and the Great Migration of 1916–1918," *Social Problems*, Vol. 31, No. 1 (October 1983), pp. 73–83; Theodore Kornweibel, Jr., *Railroads in the African American Experience: A Photographic Journey* (Baltimore: Johns Hopkins University Press, 2010), pp. 174–180; Peter Gottlieb, *Making Their Own Way: Southern Blacks' Migration to Pittsburgh, 1916–1930* (Urbana: University of Illinois Press, 1987), pp. 55–59; Sean Dennis Cashman, *America in the Twenties and Thirties: The Olympian Age of Franklin Delano Roosevelt* (New York: New York University Press, 1989), p. 267.

89. August Meier and Elliott Rudwick, *Black Detroit and the Rise of the UAW* (New York: Oxford University Press, 1979), pp. 9–11; Milton C. Sernett, *Bound for the Promised Land: African American Religion and the Great Migration* (Durham: Duke University Press, 1997), pp. 148–149.

Chapter 4: The World of Numbers

1. United States Commission on Civil Rights, *Civil Rights and the Mortgage Crisis* (Washington: U.S. Commission on Civil Rights, 2009), p. 53.

2. Ibid. See also page 61; Robert B. Avery and Glenn B. Canner, "New Information Reported under HMDA and Its Application in Fair Lending Enforcement," *Federal Reserve Bulletin*, Summer 2005, p. 379; Wilhelmina A.

Leigh and Danielle Huff, "African Americans and Homeownership: The Subprime Lending Experience, 1995 to 2007," *Joint Center for Political and Economic Studies*, November 2007, p. 5.

3. Jim Wooten, "Answers to Credit Woes are Not in Black and White," *Atlanta Journal-Constitution*, November 6, 2007, p. 12A.

4. Harold A. Black, M. Cary Collins and Ken B. Cyree, "Do Black-Owned Banks Discriminate Against Black Borrowers?" *Journal of Financial Services Research*, Vol. 11, Issue 1–2 (February 1997), pp. 189–204.

5. Robert Rector and Rea S. Hederman, "Two Americas: One Rich, One Poor? Understanding Income Inequality in the United States," Heritage Foundation *Backgrounder*, No. 1791 (August 24, 2004), pp. 7, 8.

6. The number of people in the various quintiles in 2015 was computed by multiplying the number of "consumer units" in each quintile by the average number of people per consumer unit. See Table 1 in Veri Crain and Taylor J. Wilson, "Use with Caution: Interpreting Consumer Expenditure Income Group Data," *Beyond the Numbers* (Washington: U.S. Bureau of Labor Statistics, May 2017), p. 3.

7. Ibid.

8. Herman P. Miller, *Income Distribution in the United States* (Washington: U.S. Department of Commerce, Bureau of the Census, 1966), p. 7.

9. Rose M. Kreider and Diana B. Elliott, "America's Family and Living Arrangements: 2007," *Current Population Reports*, P20–561 (Washington: U.S. Bureau of the Census, 2009), p. 5.

10. W. Michael Cox and Richard Alm, "By Our Own Bootstraps: Economic Opportunity & the Dynamics of Income Distribution," *Annual Report, 1995*, Federal Reserve Bank of Dallas, p. 8.

11. Richard V. Reeves, "Stop Pretending You're Not Rich," *New York Times*, June 11, 2017, Sunday Review section, p. 5.

12. Mark Robert Rank, Thomas A. Hirschl and Kirk A. Foster, *Chasing the American Dream: Understanding What Shapes Our Fortunes* (Oxford: Oxford University Press, 2014), p. 105.

13. U.S. Department of the Treasury, "Income Mobility in the U.S. from 1996 to 2005," November 13, 2007, pp. 2, 4, 7.

14. Ibid., pp. 2, 4; Internal Revenue Service, "The 400 Individual Income Tax Returns Reporting the Highest Adjusted Gross Incomes Each Year, 1992–2000," *Statistics of Income Bulletin*, Spring 2003, Publication 1136 (Revised 6–03), p. 7.
15. Heather Mac Donald, *Are Cops Racist? How the War Against the Police Harms Black Americans* (Chicago: Ivan R. Dee, 2003), pp. 28, 31, 32.
16. Ibid., pp. 28–34.
17.

GROUPS	MEDIAN AGE
Black	33.2
Cambodian	31.6
Chinese	38.2
Cuban	40.4
Japanese	49.6
Mexican	26.4
Puerto Rican	29.0
White	40.3
TOTAL POPULATION	37.6

Source: U.S. Census Bureau, B01002, Median Age by Sex, Universe: Total Population, 2011–2015 American Community Survey Selected Population Tables.
18. Heather Mac Donald, *Are Cops Racist?*, p. 29.
19. Heather Mac Donald, *The War on Cops: How the New Attack on Law and Order Makes Everyone Less Safe* (New York: Encounter Books, 2016), pp. 56–57, 69–71.
20. Sterling A. Brown, *A Son's Return: Selected Essays of Sterling A. Brown*, edited by Mark A. Sanders (Boston: Northeastern University Press, 1996), p. 73.
21. Mark Robert Rank, Thomas A. Hirschl and Kirk A. Foster, *Chasing the American Dream*, p. 97.

22. Internal Revenue Service, "The 400 Individual Income Tax Returns Reporting the Highest Adjusted Gross Incomes Each Year, 1992–2000," *Statistics of Income Bulletin*, Spring 2003, Publication 1136 (Revised 6–03), p. 7.

23. With nine people who are transients in the higher bracket for just one year out of a decade, that means that 90 transients will be in that bracket during that decade. The one person who is in that higher income bracket in every year of the decade brings the total number of people in the income bracket at some point during the decade to 91. The transients' total income for that decade, which was $12.6 million for the initial 9 transients, adds up to $126 million for all 90 transients who spent a year each in the higher bracket. When the $5 million earned by the one person who was in the higher bracket for all ten years of the decade is added, that makes $131 million for all 91 people who were in the higher bracket at some point during the course of the decade. These 91 people thus have an average annual income of $143,956.04— which is less than three times the average annual income of the 10 people who earned $50,000 a year.

24. See data and documentation in Thomas Sowell, *Wealth, Poverty and Politics*, revised and enlarged edition (New York: Basic Books, 2016), pp. 321–322.

25. William Julius Wilson, *When Work Disappears: The World of the New Urban Poor* (New York: Alfred A. Knopf, 1996), p. xix.

26. Ibid., p. 67.

27. Ibid., p. 140.

28. Ibid., pp. 178, 179.

29. David Caplovitz, *The Poor Pay More: Consumer Practices of Low-Income Families* (New York: The Free Press, 1967), pp. 94–95.

30. J.D. Vance, *Hillbilly Elegy: A Memoir of a Family and Culture in Crisis* (New York: HarperCollins, 2016), p. 93.

31. Ibid., p. 57.

32. Ibid.

33. John U. Ogbu, *Black American Students in an Affluent Suburb: A Study of Academic Disengagement* (Mahwah, New Jersey: Lawrence Erlbaum Associates, 2003), pp. 15, 17, 21, 28, 240.

34. Richard Lynn, *The Global Bell Curve: Race, IQ, and Inequality Worldwide* (Augusta, Georgia: Washington Summit Publishers, 2008), p. 51.

35. James Bartholomew, *The Welfare of Nations* (Washington: The Cato Institute, 2016), pp. 104–106.

36. Michael A. Fletcher and Jonathan Weisman, "Bush Supports Democrats' Minimum Wage Hike Plan," *Washington Post*, December 21, 2006, p. A14.

37. "Labours Lost," *The Economist*, July 15, 2000, pp. 64–65; Robert W. Van Giezen, "Occupational Wages in the Fast-Food Restaurant Industry," *Monthly Labor Review*, August 1994, pp. 24–30.

38. "Labours Lost," *The Economist*, July 15, 2000, pp. 64–65.

39. Richard A. Lester, "Shortcomings of Marginal Analysis for Wage-Employment Problems," *American Economic Review*, Vol. 36, No. 1 (March 1946), pp. 63–82.

40. David Card and Alan B. Krueger, "Minimum Wages and Employment: A Case Study of the Fast-Food Industry in New Jersey and Pennsylvania," *American Economic Review*, Vol. 84, No. 4 (September 1994), pp. 772–793; David Card and Alan B. Krueger, *Myth and Measurement: The New Economics of the Minimum Wage* (Princeton: Princeton University Press, 1995); Douglas K. Adie, Book Review, "Myth and Measurement: The New Economics of the Minimum Wage," *Cato Journal*, Vol. 15, No. 1 (Spring/Summer 1995), pp. 137–140.

41. Richard B. Berman, "Dog Bites Man: Minimum Wage Hikes Still Hurt," *Wall Street Journal*, March 29, 1995, p. A12; "Testimony of Richard B. Berman," *Evidence Against a Higher Minimum Wage*, Hearing Before the Joint Economic Committee, Congress of the United States, One Hundred Fourth Congress, first session, April 5, 1995, Part II, pp. 12–13; Gary S. Becker, "It's Simple: Hike the Minimum Wage, and You Put People Out of Work," *BusinessWeek*, March 6, 1995, p. 22; Paul Craig Roberts, "A Minimum-Wage Study with Minimum Credibility," *BusinessWeek*, April 24, 1995, p. 22.

42. Dara Lee Luca and Michael Luca, "Survival of the Fittest: The Impact of the Minimum Wage on Firm Exit," Harvard Business School, Working Paper 17–088, 2017, pp. 1, 2, 3, 10.

43. Don Watkins and Yaron Brook, *Equal Is Unfair: America's Misguided Fight Against Income Inequality* (New York: St. Martin's Press, 2016), p. 125.

44. Ekaterina Jardim, et al., "Minimum Wage Increases, Wages, and Low-Wage Employment: Evidence from Seattle," Working Paper Number 23532,

"Abstract" (Cambridge, Massachusetts: National Bureau of Economic Research, June 2017).

45. "Economic and Financial Indicators," *The Economist*, March 15, 2003, p. 100.
46. "Economic and Financial Indicators," *The Economist*, March 2, 2013, p. 88.
47. "Economic and Financial Indicators," *The Economist*, September 7, 2013, p. 92.
48. "Hong Kong's Jobless Rate Falls," *Wall Street Journal*, January 16, 1991, p. C16.
49. U. S. Bureau of the Census, *Historical Statistics of the United States: Colonial Times to 1970* (Washington: Government Printing Office, 1975), Part 1, p. 126.
50. Burton W. Fulsom, Jr., *The Myth of the Robber Barons: A New Look at the Rise of Big Business in America*, sixth edition (Herndon, Virginia: Young America's Foundation, 2010), pp. 108, 109, 115, 116.
51. Ibid., p. 116.
52. Alan Reynolds, "Why 70% Tax Rates Won't Work," *Wall Street Journal*, June 16, 2011, p. A19; Stephen Moore, "Real Tax Cuts Have Curves," *Wall Street Journal*, June 13, 2005, p. A13.
53. Edmund L. Andrews, "Surprising Jump in Tax Revenues Curbs U.S. Deficit," *New York Times*, July 9, 2006, p. A1.
54. Ekaterina Jardim, et al., "Minimum Wage Increases, Wages, and Low-Wage Employment: Evidence from Seattle," Working Paper Number 23532, "Abstract" (Cambridge, Massachusetts: National Bureau of Economic Research, June 2017).

Chapter 5: Social Visions and Human Consequences

1. Gabriel Tortella, "Patterns of Economic Retardation and Recovery in South-Western Europe in the Nineteenth and Twentieth Centuries," *Economic History Review*, Vol. 47, No. 1 (February 1994), p. 2.
2. Steven Pinker, *The Better Angels of Our Nature: Why Violence Has Declined* (New York: Viking, 2011), pp. 85–87, 93–104.
3. Darrel Hess, *McKnight's Physical Geography: A Landscape Appreciation*, eleventh edition (Boston: Pearson Education, Inc., 2014), p. 198.
4. T. Scott Bryan, *The Geysers of Yellowstone*, fourth edition (Boulder: University of Colorado Press, 2008), pp. 9–10, 406–407.

5.   *The World Almanac and Book of Facts: 2017* (New York: World Almanac Books, 2017), pp. 687, 688.

6.   Documented examples can be found in my *The Vision of the Anointed: Self-Congratulation as a Basis for Social Policy* (New York: Basic Books, 1995), pp. 35–37 and *Intellectuals and Society,* second edition (New York: Basic Books, 2012), pp. 116–119. Isolated examples have appeared in my *Conquests and Cultures: An International History* (New York: Basic Books, 1998), pp. 125, 210, 217 and *Migrations and Cultures: A World View* (New York: Basic Books, 1996), pp. 4, 17, 31, 57, 123, 130, 135, 152, 154, 157, 176, 179, 193, 196, 211, 265, 277, 278, 289, 297, 298, 300, 320, 345–346, 353–354, 355, 358, 366, 372–373.

7.   The Economist, *Pocket World in Figures: 2017 edition* (London: Profile Books, 2016), p. 18.

8.   Bureau of Justice Statistics, *Survey of State Prison Inmates, 1991* (Washington: U.S. Department of Justice, 1993), p. 9.

9.   Malcolm Gladwell, *Outliers: The Story of Success* (New York: Little, Brown and Company, 2008), pp. 111–113.

10. Oliver MacDonagh, "The Irish Famine Emigration to the United States," *Perspectives in American History,* Vol. X (1976), p. 405; Thomas Bartlett, *Ireland: A History* (New York: Cambridge University Press, 2010), p. 284.

11. W.E. Vaughan and A.J. Fitzpatrick, editors, *Irish Historical Statistics: Population, 1821–1971* (Dublin: Royal Irish Academy, 1978), pp. 260–261.

12. Tyler Anbinder, *City of Dreams: The 400-Year Epic History of Immigrant New York* (Boston: Houghton Mifflin Harcourt, 2016), p. 127.

13. See, for example, Jason L. Riley, *Please Stop Helping Us: How Liberals Make It Harder for Blacks to Succeed* (New York: Encounter Books, 2014), pp. 42–43; "Now D.C. Bans Suspensions as Racist," *Investor's Business Daily,* July 18, 2014, p. A14; "Classrooms Run by the Unsuspended," *Investor's Business Daily,* July 3, 2014, p. A14; Paul Sperry, "AG Holder Urges Schools to Go Easy on Discipline," *Investor's Business Daily,* January 9, 2014, p. A1; Eva S. Moskowitz, "Turning Schools Into Fight Clubs," *Wall Street Journal,* April 2, 2015, p. A15. See also Theodore Dalrymple, *Life at the Bottom: The Worldview That Makes the Underclass* (Chicago: Ivan R. Dee, 2001), pp. 68–69; James Bartholomew, *The Welfare of Nations* (Washington: The Cato Institute, 2016), p. 103.

14. Nina Easton, "Class, Reimagined," *Fortune*, March 15, 2015, p. 34; Daniel Bergner, "Class Warfare," *New York Times Magazine*, September 7, 2014, pp. 60–68; Jay Mathews, "KIPP Continues to Break the Mold and Garner Excellent Results," *Washington Post*, February 3, 2014, p. B2; Jay Mathews, "Five-Year Study Concludes that KIPP Student Gains Are Substantial," *Washington Post*, March 2, 2013, p. B2; *KIPP: 2014 Report Card* (San Francisco: KIPP Foundation, 2014), pp. 10, 19.

15. James Bartholomew, *The Welfare of Nations*, p. 103.

16. Ibid., p. 92.

17. "The World's Billionaires," *Forbes*, March 28, 2017, pp. 84–85. V.I. Lenin tried to rescue Marxist theory by claiming that rich countries exploited poor countries, and shared some of their "super-profits" with their own working classes, in order to stave off revolution. But in fact most rich countries' international investments are concentrated in other rich countries, with their investments in poor countries being a very small fraction of their foreign investments and their incomes from these investments in poor countries being a very small fraction of their total income from foreign investments. See my *Wealth, Poverty and Politics*, revised and enlarged edition (New York: Basic Books, 2016) pp. 245–247.

18. For documented specifics, see my *Wealth, Poverty and Politics*, revised and enlarged edition, p. 136.

19. See, for example, hostile responses to empirical data from Daniel Patrick Moynihan, James S. Coleman, Jay Belsky and Heather Mac Donald in Jean M. White, "Moynihan Report Criticized as 'Racist,'" *Washington Post*, November 22, 1965, p. A3; William Ryan, "Savage Discovery: The Moynihan Report," *The Nation*, November 22, 1965, pp. 380–384; Diane Ravitch, "The Coleman Reports and American Education," *Social Theory and Social Policy: Essays in Honor of James S. Coleman*, edited by Aage B. Sorenson and Seymour Spilerman (Westport, Connecticut: Praeger, 1993), pp. 129–141; James Bartholomew, *The Welfare of Nations*, pp. 174–175; Tim Lynch, "There Is No War on Cops," *Reason*, August/September 2016, pp. 58–61; William McGurn, "The Silencing of Heather Mac Donald," *Wall Street Journal*, April 11, 2017, p. A15.

20. "Bicker Warning," *The Economist*, April 1, 2017, p. 23.

21. Theodore Dalrymple, *Life at the Bottom*, p. 6.

22. Barry Latzer, *The Rise and Fall of Violent Crime in America* (New York: Encounter Books, 2016), p. 19; *Today's VD Control Problem: Joint Statement by The American Public Health Association, The American Social Health Association, The American Venereal Disease Association, The Association of State and Territorial Health Officers in co-operation with The American Medical Association*, February 1966, p. 20; Hearings Before the Select Committee on Population, Ninety-Fifth Congress, Second Session, *Fertility and Contraception in America: Adolescent and Pre-Adolescent Pregnancy* (Washington: U.S. Government Printing Office, 1978), Volume II, p. 625; Jacqueline R. Kasun, *The War Against Population: The Economics and Ideology of World Population Control* (San Francisco: Ignatius Press, 1988), pp. 142, 143, 144; Sally Curtin, et al., "2010 Pregnancy Rates Among U.S. Women," *National Center for Health Statistics*, December 2015, p. 6.

23. U.S. Bureau of the Census, *Historical Statistics of the United States: Colonial Times to 1970* (Washington: Government Printing Office, 1975), Part I, p. 414.

24. Stephan Thernstrom and Abigail Thernstrom, *America in Black and White: One Nation, Indivisible* (New York: Simon & Schuster, 1997), p. 262.

25. Steven Pinker, *The Better Angels of Our Nature*, pp. 106–107.

26. John Kenneth Galbraith, *The Selected Letters of John Kenneth Galbraith*, edited by Richard P.F. Holt (Cambridge: Cambridge University Press, 2017), p. 47.

27. James Bartholomew, *The Welfare of Nations*, pp. 187–189.

28. Joyce Lee Malcolm, *Guns and Violence: The English Experience* (Cambridge, Massachusetts: Harvard University Press, 2002), p. 168.

29. See, for example, Sean O'Neill and Fiona Hamilton, "Mobs Rule as Police Surrender Streets," *The Times* (London), August 9, 2011, pp. 1, 5; Martin Beckford, et al., "Carry On Looting," *The Daily Telegraph* (London), August 8, 2011, pp. 1, 2; Philip Johnston, "The Long Retreat of Order," *The Daily Telegraph* (London), August 10, 2011, p. 19; Alistair MacDonald and Guy Chazan, "World News: Britain Tallies Damage and Sets Out Anti-Riot Steps," *Wall Street Journal*, August 12, 2011, p. A6.

30. Theodore Dalrymple, *Life at the Bottom*, pp. 136–139; James Bartholomew, *The Welfare of Nations*, p. 203.

31. Stephan Thernstrom and Abigail Thernstrom, *America in Black and White*, p. 238.

32. Ibid., p. 237.

33. Charles Murray, *Coming Apart: The State of White America: 1960–2010* (New York: Crown Forum, 2012), pp. 160, 161.

34. James Bartholomew, *The Welfare of Nations*, p. 164.

35. For documentation, see Thomas Sowell, *Inside American Education: The Decline, the Deception, the Dogmas* (New York: Free Press, 1993), Chapter 1.

36. E.W. Kenworthy, "Action by Senate: Revised Measure Now Goes Back to House for Concurrence," *New York Times*, June 20, 1964, p. 1; "House Civil Rights Vote," *New York Times*, July 3, 1964, p. 9; E.W. Kenworthy, "Voting Measure Passed by House," *New York Times*, August 4, 1965, pp. 1, 17; "Vote Rights Bill: Senate Sends Measure to LBJ," *Los Angeles Times*, August 5, 1965, p. 1.

37. Steven Pinker, *The Better Angels of Our Nature*, pp. 106–116. In addition to statistical evidence, eye-witness accounts show the same degeneration on both sides of the Atlantic. See, for example, Theodore Dalrymple, *Life at the Bottom*, pp. x, xi, 45, 67, 72, 139, 153, 166, 181, 188, 223–225; J.D. Vance, *Hillbilly Elegy: A Memoir of a Family and Culture in Crisis* (New York: HarperCollins, 2016), pp. 20–22, 49–50, 51; Charles Murray, *Coming Apart*, pp. 167, 210–220, 271–272. These accounts of trends among the white underclass show a great similarity to many well-known trends among the black underclass.

38. Shelby Steele, *White Guilt: How Blacks and Whites Together Destroyed the Promise of the Civil Rights Era* (New York: HarperCollins Publishers, 2006), p. 123.

39. Ibid., p. 124.

40. Stephan Thernstrom and Abigail Thernstrom, *America in Black and White*, pp. 233–234.

41. James Bartholomew, *The Welfare of Nations*, p. 195.

42. David Cole, "Can Our Shameful Prisons Be Reformed?" *New York Review of Books*, November 19, 2009, p. 41.

43. James Bartholomew, *The Welfare of Nations*, p. 195.

44. John McWhorter, *Talking Back, Talking Black: Truths About America's Lingua Franca* (New York: Bellevue Literary Press, 2017), p. 11.

45. Ibid., pp. 98–101.

46. Ibid., p. 12.

47. Ibid., p. 13.

48. Ibid., p. 12.

49. His book, *Talking Back, Talking Black* includes this dedication:

> For Vanessa Hamilton McWhorter, who came into this world, born reflective, while I was writing this book.
>
> I hope that she will read this as soon as she is old enough to take it in, to make sure she never for a second thinks black people's speech is full of mistakes.
>
> And for my cousin Octavia Thompson, who speaks what I think of as the perfect Black English, which I dare anybody to diss.

50. Derek Sayer, *The Coasts of Bohemia: A Czech History* (Princeton: Princeton University Press, 1998), p. 90.

51. Melanie Kirkpatrick, "Business in a Common Tongue," *Wall Street Journal*, August 28, 2017, p. A15.

52. David Deterding, *Singapore English* (Edinburgh: Edinburgh University Press, 2007), pp. 4–5; Sandra L. Suárez, "Does English Rule? Language Instruction and Economic Strategies in Singapore, Ireland, and Puerto Rico," *Comparative Politics*, Vol. 37, No. 4 (July 2005), pp. 465, 467–468.

53. Lawrence E. Harrison, *The Pan-American Dream: Do Latin America's Cultural Values Discourage True Partnership with the United States and Canada?* (New York: Basic Books, 1997), p. 207.

54. Jeffrey D. Sachs, *The Age of Sustainable Development* (New York: Columbia University Press, 2015), p. 56.

55. Aaron E. Carroll, "Limiting Food Stamp Choices Can Help Fight Obesity," *New York Times*, September 27, 2016, p. A3; Robert Paarlberg, "Obesity: The New Hunger," *Wall Street Journal*, May 11, 2016, p. A11; James A. Levine, "Poverty and Obesity in the U.S.," *Diabetes*, Vol. 60 (November 2011), pp. 2667–2668; Sabrina Tavernise, "Study Finds Modest Declines in Obesity Rates Among Young Children from Poor Families," *New York Times*, December 26, 2012, p. A18; Associated Press, "Obesity Grows Among the Affluent," *Wall Street Journal*, May 3, 2005, p. D4.

56. Annie Sciacca, "6-Figure Earnings Now 'Low Income' in Marin and SF," *Marin Independent Journal*, April 23, 2017, p. 1.

57. E. Franklin Frazier, "Negro Harlem: An Ecological Study," *American Journal of Sociology*, Vol. 43, No. 1 (July 1937), pp. 72–88; reprinted in *E. Franklin Frazier on Race Relations: Selected Writings*, edited by G. Franklin Edwards (Chicago: University of Chicago Press, 1968), pp. 142–160.

58. G. Franklin Edwards, editor, *E. Franklin Frazier on Race Relations*, pp. 148, 149, 152, 157, 158.

59. "Going Global," *The Economist*, December 19, 2015, p. 107.

60. Amy Chua and Jed Rubenfeld, *The Triple Package: How Three Unlikely Traits Explain the Rise and Fall of Cultural Groups in America* (New York: The Penguin Press, 2014), p. 39.

61. Warren C. Scoville, *The Persecution of Huguenots and French Economic Development: 1680–1720* (Berkeley: University of California Press, 1960), Chapters VI–X.

62. Kevin D. Williamson, *What Doomed Detroit?*, Encounter Broadside No. 37 (New York: Encounter Books, 2013).

63. See, for example, Orlando Patterson, *Slavery and Social Death: A Comparative Study* (Cambridge, Massachusetts: Harvard University Press, 1982), p. 176; Stanley L. Engerman, *Slavery, Emancipation & Freedom: Comparative Perspectives* (Baton Rouge: Louisiana State University Press, 2007), pp. 3, 4; William D. Phillips, Jr., *Slavery from Roman Times to the Early Transatlantic Trade* (Minneapolis: University of Minnesota Press, 1985), pp. 46, 47; Ellen Churchill Semple, *Influences of Geographic Environment* (New York: Henry Holt and Company, 1911), p. 90; R.W. Beachey, *The Slave Trade of Eastern Africa* (New York: Barnes & Noble Books, 1976), p. 182; Harold D. Nelson, et al., *Nigeria: A Country Study* (Washington: U.S. Government Printing Office, 1982), p. 16; Christina Snyder, *Slavery in Indian Country: The Changing Face of Captivity in Early America* (Cambridge, Massachusetts: Harvard University Press, 2010), pp. 4, 5; T'ung-tsu Ch'ü, *Han Social Structure*, edited by Jack L. Dull (Seattle: University of Washington Press, 1972), pp. 140–141.

64. Robert C. Davis, *Christian Slaves, Muslim Masters: White Slavery in the Mediterranean, the Barbary Coast, and Italy, 1500–1800* (New York: Palgrave

Macmillan, 2003), p. 23; Philip D. Curtin, *The Atlantic Slave Trade: A Census* (Madison: University of Wisconsin Press, 1969), pp. 72, 75, 87.

65. An essay on this subject can be found in my *Black Rednecks and White Liberals* (San Francisco: Encounter Books, 2005), pp. 111–169.

66. Edmund Burke, *Reflections on the Revolution in France and Other Writings*, edited by Jesse Norman (New York: Alfred A. Knopf, 2015), p. 549.

INDEX

INDEX